"One of my favorite passages in the Bible is the Book of Nehemiah. Kevin and Steven have taken this passage and pulled some timeless money-management principles from it. I know that God's Word, when it comes to finances, is always right, always relevant, and will never change. This book will help you apply God's transcendent, practical, and wise principles to your financial life. I endorse it enthusiastically."

Ron Blue, President
Kingdom Advisors

"Kevin Cross has written a truly inspirational book for those who face financial difficulties. Based on the Book of Nehemiah, this practical book addresses what God has to say about money and its purposes. He clearly demonstrates how trusting God is the key to becoming debt-free and enjoying purposeful living. I heartily recommend this book. Follow its principles and your financial fortress will remain secure even in difficult economic times."

Howard Dayton
Cofounder of Crown Financial Ministries and author
of numerous books on biblical money management

"Wonderfully written, different from other financial books. Touching examples of real life—Kevin's life and the woman who wanted a BMW are must reads!"

Melinda McClusky
South Florida grandmother

"Kevin, thank you for allowing God to use you. Your willingness to make a change in people's lives has changed my life!"

Judy "K" (Karagiannes)
(See Day 45)

Building Your
Financial
Fortress in
52 Days

The Lessons of Nehemiah

Kevin Cross, CPA

with Steven White

Bridge-Logos

Alachua, Florida 32615

Bridge-Logos

Alachua, FL 32615 USA

Building Your Financial Fortress in 52 Days
by Kevin Cross
with Steven White

Copyright ©2009 by Bridge-Logos

Printed in the United States of America.

Library of Congress Catalog Card Number: pending
International Standard Book Number 978-0-88270-643-6

G218.316.N.m812.35240

Introduction

Nehemiah's story begs to be told with all of its financial wisdom and the rich morsels of managing money God's way. This book is unlike any other book on finances, self-help, or even motivation ever written, but it certainly speaks directly and compassionately to these vital subjects. This book will take the world's faulty definition of success and turn it inside out. There will be quotes by people whose entire philosophies are not biblical, but may shed some light, or at least humor, on the subject. It will challenge you to upgrade your financial goals, deepen your desires, and give you a hope that far outweighs the temporary happiness found in spending money on earthly endeavors.

The Book of Nehemiah was written about 2500 years ago, in approximately 445 B.C. This is an historical account of a courageous man who had much to lose in terms of his stable and comfortable life. He chose to honor God by being used to save a remnant of God's chosen people and the city of Jerusalem, which was nearly destroyed, and rebuild both the people and the city in fifty-two days.

Building a financial fortress may not be an entirely accurate term for some people. Maybe you have experienced a financial disaster that requires complete bulldozing and rebuilding. Or you may be looking toward retirement and just need sage advice. While others may have a decade or two of peak earning years left and would like a fresh perspective. Still others may be at the halftime in life and want to not only finish well, but also have the second half be so intentionally invested that only death itself will prevent it from happening.

You may be looking to rebuild your wall much like Nehemiah did with the blessing and help of God. That is where most of us are, and that is where God wants to meet you and "give you hope and a future."[1] The choice is ours. We can choose to continue to manage our finances our way and reap heartache and discontent or we can choose to do it God's way.

Take fifty-two days to read this book—one *day* at a time. Ponder the truths set forth, don't read too fast, and let God speak to your heart the things He wants you to know about your own personal fortress. If we do it His way, He promises that we will be the recipients of *all* joy and peace, only "as we trust in Him."[2]

DAY 1

The Encounter

" ... HANANI, ONE OF MY BROTHERS, CAME FROM JUDAH WITH SOME
OTHER MEN, AND I QUESTIONED THEM ABOUT THE JEWISH REMNANT
THAT SURVIVED THE EXILE, AND ALSO ABOUT JERUSALEM. THEY SAID TO
ME, 'THOSE WHO SURVIVED THE EXILE AND ARE BACK IN THE PROVINCE
ARE IN GREAT TROUBLE AND DISGRACE. THE WALL OF JERUSALEM
IS BROKEN DOWN, AND ITS GATES HAVE BEEN BURNED WITH FIRE'"
(NEHEMIAH 1:2-3).

"NOTHING WILL SHAKE A MAN—OR AT ANY RATE, A MAN LIKE ME—OUT
OF HIS MERELY VERBAL THINKING AND HIS MERELY NOTIONAL BELIEFS.
HE HAS TO BE KNOCKED SILLY BEFORE HE COMES TO HIS SENSES."
– C.S. LEWIS

"SOME MEN WORSHIP RANK, SOME WORSHIP HEROES, SOME WORSHIP
POWER, SOME WORSHIP GOD, AND OVER THESE IDEALS THEY DISPUTE,
BUT THEY ALL WORSHIP MONEY." – MARK TWAIN

Nehemiah led a comfortable life. He held a stately position in
the most powerful kingdom on Earth. He owned a beautiful
house near the palace of Shushan with a pool shaded from
the afternoon sun by giant palms and where breezes gently crept
over the waters in the summer months, making the Persian heat
bearable. He would pass entire days luxuriating in his floating
lounger and sipping those little drinks with the pink umbrellas
in them. He was wealthy, content, and well fed. As the king's
cupbearer, Nehemiah was charged with the vital task of tasting
King Artaxerxes's wine to make sure it was not poisoned.

Though this might appear to be a risky and thankless position, it was actually highly coveted and it permitted intimate access to the king and required his utmost trust. As such, the king and Nehemiah grew close and he reaped the many benefits such a relationship offers.

One can imagine Nehemiah's struggle, then, when his brother Hanani and some friends came over for a chat. It started innocently enough when Nehemiah casually asked his brother, "What of our people and the city where we used to live?"

The answer his brother gave changed everything. Nehemiah's brother said, to paraphrase, "Our people are being beaten up and taken advantage of once again, and the neighborhood we lived in looks like a bomb hit it." The news of the mournful and desolate condition of Jerusalem wounded Nehemiah deeply. What started as just the guys hanging out, perhaps playing golf or tennis or watching Sunday football, turned ugly. This exchange, though, brought greater gain, greater meaning, and greater reward than any other single meeting he had ever had. Nehemiah was more than destined for this moment; he was created for it. But he was not prepared for it.

You see, this is your moment—your time not just to seize the day, but to rise to the occasion. Yes, *you*! Not just the person who may buy this book, but *you*—the person reading this in the airport, on the plane, in the office, or maybe over someone's shoulder. Yes, you. We are never completely prepared for the defining moments of life. Until then we may wonder and wander from book to book, resolution to resolution, diet to diet, and budget to budget, never finding our way. We only settle for things that substitute or distract us from the goal of intense financial satisfaction.

If you are burnt out on the world's empty philosophy on money, upgrade today to God's view of money. Even though we will be focusing on the life of Governor Nehemiah and his financial decisions, convictions, and heart changes along the way, the rest of God's Word speaks about money and possessions over 2,350 times.[3] Most are warnings or instructions on how not to mishandle money in order to avoid financial pain. When Larry Burkett, the founder of Christian Financial Concepts, now Crown Financial Ministries, was alive and teaching this message, he loved to quote a saying by the wealthiest and wisest man who ever lived—Solomon: "It is the blessing of the Lord that brings wealth and He adds no trouble to it."[4]

The amount you have been entrusted with, whether it is $500 a month or $500 an hour, is a blessing from God and He will add no trouble or sorrow to it if you choose to use it His way. Why? Is He a showboat, glory hog, or a self-consumed egotistical cosmic Darth Vader? No. He genuinely cares about us so much more than we can possibly comprehend and wants to save us from the heartache that lies in wait for us when we do it our way. Since God has proven His love for us by dying, coming back to life, and promising to always be with us and never replace us with another love, then we can and should trust Him with something comparatively minor: our finances.

This book is about the financial life that God wants to give us—one of great joy and peace. It is a financial life that bears no scars from the wounds inflicted by the world's ways. One that will speak silently of the hope God has infused into us to pour into the lives of others so that they may experience the depth and intense pleasure of His love in their lives. In Romans 15:13, He tells us this through Paul, the Jewish Pharisee-turned-follower: "May the God of hope fill you with all joy and peace as you trust in him, so that you may overflow with hope by the power of the Holy Spirit." The great news is that you don't have to be a financial guru, a bean counter, or even a bookkeeper.

God empowers you to do great things in the area of money and as a result He is glorified and we get all the joy. What an incredible concept! He gets the credit, more peoples' lives change, and we receive that most coveted and illusive lifetime quest, joy and peace. Money can't buy it, but it is attainable with God's currency.

This is not a book on finance, management, or leadership. This book is about building enough margin in your life to glean real meaning from its intended use.

Nehemiah's financial choices made him one of the finest financial role models in the ancient Scriptures. Applying these financial principles and convictions will give you the bricks and mortar to construct your financial fortress.

DAY 2

The Heartbreak

"WHEN I HEARD THESE THINGS, I SAT DOWN AND WEPT ..."
(NEHEMIAH 1:4).

"[PAIN] REMOVES THE VEIL; IT PLANTS THE FLAG OF TRUTH WITHIN THE
FORTRESS OF A REBEL SOUL." – C.S. LEWIS

"THROUGHOUT HISTORY THE MOST UNIVERSALLY ACKNOWLEDGED
PROBLEM WITH MONEY IS THAT ITS PURSUIT IS INSATIABLE."
– OS GUINNESS

Nehemiah wept in front of his brother and friends. That is not a manly thing to do. At least, that is what society tells us. Sure, women do it. They show emotion with their girlfriends, their husbands, and their children. They show emotion watching movies, reading a good book, or a bad novel. They show emotion when they are sad, mad, happy, and in-between. We men are woefully inexperienced and frankly are novices at the fine art of crying. Nehemiah let it go because the stakes were so high.

Now fast-forward 2500 years. Your financial fortress is in ruin. Actually, you might describe your situation as a financial house of cards or financial failure. Or the financial facade in which many are living—the life of plastic[5] or the mortgage debacle—that's the place where you may find yourself owing more than what your home is worth. It is the evidence that convicts people of spending tomorrow's earnings today.

Presuming on the future—that was the elaborate plan that included a safety net just in case the money acquired from borrowing and overextending ran out. However, that safety net was merely an illusion of smoke and mirrors. It was the option that any of us could, at any time, "flip," "dump," "liquidate," "rent," or otherwise convert our stuff into a handsome gain that would, in turn, pay off all of our mortgages, auto loans, credit lines, credit cards, personal loans, student loans, paycheck loans, construction loans, margin loans, or any other creative way we were deceived.

The flash, not the cash, is many peoples' mantra (unless it is a cash advance). The reality of literally living paycheck to paycheck, one check from being homeless if it were not for more plastic or credit lines or the ever-so-popular refinancing windfall that gives the debtor a false sense of security until the next adjustable rate mortgage increase.

Our pain is twenty-first century, but God's plan is as old as time. Nehemiah more than felt the pain. He became it. His life came crashing to a halt. No longer did any of the baloney of the world matter—the things, the money, the position, the praise; not even the joy mattered any longer. He was face-to-face with the question, "Do I live or do I rot on this vine I find myself on?"

You and I have been there. Perhaps you are there right now—at the crossroads, at the end of your rope, surrendered to anything, blissfully ignorant in the lifeless, joyless life you have settled for.

The year was 1988. I found myself in Florida, in a state-of-the-art jail cell with the murderer of three people at Wendy's. I was a twenty-one-year-old corporate embezzler, not the violent criminal he was. I could see the guards chuckling as I turned and looked with fear and trembling as they slammed and locked the cell door. I was still wondering why this happened and how I got caught and when my law school study partners were going to spring me. I couldn't help but be scared. Fear of the unknown is devastating.

I had been a Christian since I was very young, but could not see the logic or the pleasure in living a non-hypocritical life. Religion had its place and God's Word was clear about how to avoid eternal hell, but I felt I was on my own with the rest—until that first night in the jail cell with the Wendy's murderer.[6]

It was the get-rich-at-any-cost 1980's I found myself in, and I loved what it meant. Fast tracking to *real* success—that insatiable appetite for the lifestyle of excess and indulgence.

I knew accounting and law would fast-pass me to great comfort. I came from a middle-class family of six and felt the pangs of not having enough. I set my eyes on never feeling that pain of being *poor* again. Even though I was deceived, since most of the world would love a home, food, and fun—I was not content; thus the poverty of my soul.

After excelling in high school and getting in early to college at sixteen, my ego and my dreams were being fed. The money did not come as quickly as I desired, since college was a long haul any way you looked at it. I finished in just over three years and cheated my way into a half scholarship to law school at nineteen. But still I was not experiencing the pleasure of money. So I went with Plan B. If I couldn't get money fast enough this way, I would steal it.

You may be thinking right now, "I knew it! This is a book for financial losers." Wrong. This is a book based on a winner, and the winning practices, lifestyle, attitude, and conviction of a man who changed the world and saved many people in the process.

That man or woman could be you today. This is not another get-rich-quick, flip this property, get into multi-level marketing, offer. This is God's plan for building your financial fortress. Not a cabin or bungalow; not even a house, but a fortress that will withstand anything this life throws at you, including death.

DAY 3

The Response

" ... FOR SOME DAYS I MOURNED AND FASTED AND PRAYED BEFORE THE GOD OF HEAVEN." (NEHEMIAH 1:4)

"I NOT ONLY LIVE EACH ENDLESS DAY IN GRIEF, BUT LIVE EACH DAY THINKING ABOUT LIVING EACH DAY IN GRIEF." – C. S. LEWIS

"MONEY IS LIKE LOVE; IT KILLS SLOWLY AND PAINFULLY THE ONE WHO WITHHOLDS IT, AND ENLIVENS THE OTHER WHO TURNS IT ON HIS FELLOW MAN." – KAHLIL GIBRAN

After weeping, he prayed. Not a familiar prayer that we might pray: "O Lord, please get me out of this financial jam I am in. I promise I will never flip real estate again or gamble Or … " No, Nehemiah mourned and fasted and prayed. This could do it for many people. It is the response of a truly broken heart. David reveals this in Psalm 51:17, " … a broken spirit; a broken and contrite heart, O God, you will not despise."

You see, we must be as broken as Nehemiah and surrender our financial situation to the Creator of the Universe, and in complete humility state by our actions that the financial decisions we have made we will continue no longer. Through mourning and fasting, and great persistent prayer: "… The prayer of a righteous man is powerful and effective" (James 5:16), He will meet us, draw us near, and will begin the healing.

It only took me one night in a cell with the Wendy's murderer to bring me to the truth of Nehemiah's prayer. Unlike Nehemiah, my pain was self-inflicted. I chased the god of money and the pleasures that could be purchased. That ever-illusive hunger of my impoverished soul was my biggest secret, which was now revealed.

The Wendy's murderer and I both prayed desperate and sincere prayers that night. I remember walking into the cell and being warned with a laugh about who my cellmate was going to be. Little did I know he had been found guilty the day I became his solitary confinement buddy. What was similar in our crying out to God was that we both wanted to go back in time, get out of jail, and somehow forget the nightmare of our actions.

It was the classic jailhouse prayer. I prayed it and so do most others in my position. I knew this. My soul was bankrupt. My prayers moved from the sincere, humble, heart-wrenching, "God, rescue me" prayer, to a deeper communion and communication with God, which resulted in a face-to-face encounter that led to a subsequent "It is well with my soul" prayer. In 1873, Horatio Spafford wrote those lyrics after losing his four children, and nearly his wife, in a shipwreck. Even with great pain, his heart trusted and connected with God. That became my prayer and my hope, even though my pain was self-inflicted, and far less compared to the loss of the precious lives of loved ones. Nonetheless, I was alone, without human hope for the future. I had wounded and embarrassed my family. Now I feared for my life in a cell with a murderer.

All of my dreams had crashed and burned and all I could think about was, "Now I am the cellmate of a triple murderer who was found guilty this very day." God knew I was a bruised reed and a smoldering wick, and I was at the crossroads of my young life. In the words of the Prophet Isaiah who was not unaccustomed to difficult times himself, "A bruised reed he will not break, and a smoldering wick he will not snuff out." [7] [8]

Nehemiah chose to take the path less traveled. It was not his fight, not his life that was at stake. Maybe you feel that way today. You are successful, without financial woe at this moment, and you hope to keep it that way. This book will help you upgrade your dream, secure it, memorialize it, and pass on a legacy of the life that is truly life to your heirs or those who come after you. You may be used to save someone's financial life, or his or her marriage, or perhaps even his or her physical life. [9]

God is looking not for superstars or home run hitters or investors with a Midas touch; He is looking for faithful followers. I know it sounds too easy, but what do you have to lose? Fifty-two days of doing it God's way, as modeled by Nehemiah. If you never try it, you will always wonder what would have happened if you had. That is the life of regret. In this case, it is a life of eternal regret because the financial decisions you make today will affect not only your lifetime and the ones you love, but will affect eternity. This adds a whole new layer of urgency and seriousness to this plea for your life. It is not just about your finances.

DAY 4

The Plea

" ... O Lord, God of heaven, the great and awesome God, who keeps his covenant of love with those who love him and obey his commands ... I confess the sins we Israelites, including myself and my father's house, have committed against you."
(Nehemiah 1:5-6)

"God whispers to us in our pleasures, speaks in our conscience, but shouts in our pains: it is His megaphone to rouse a deaf world." – C.S. Lewis

"If money be not thy servant, it will be thy master. The covetous man cannot so properly be said to possess wealth, as that may be said to possess him." – Francis Bacon

When Nehemiah heard his people were in distress and his home in embers, he had a choice: blame or take charge. We are blamers. Don't get me wrong; we have good reason. Our parents, that deadbeat husband, the market—whether stock or real estate: the who's and the what's will always be there to be the focus of our blame. Nehemiah did not get angry with those wicked people or the events that caused him and his loved ones so much pain; he had a strategy. He prayed. He knew his anger would sabotage the mission if it were directed toward seeking vengeance or retaliation or worse—blaming others. Instead, he turned this great and life-changing heartache into a divine appointment with the Creator of the universe, a heart–to-heart with his heavenly King before he spoke to his earthly boss, King Artaxerxes.

He saw clearly that the situation looked hopeless and he could do nothing about it. He upgraded his existing position to a position of great strength. He beckoned the help of the One who could in fact do the incredible, the unimaginable, the truly miraculous. He chose the trail to true riches.

Imagine your situation being so imperiled that you resort to crying out to the Most High, not just once, but for many days. Add fasting to that. Then praying the prayer of a lifetime to the Creator. Nehemiah did all this and experienced miraculous results.

His humble and courageous prayer was one of a lifetime. Not the prayer made at meal times to bless the meatloaf. Or the "Now I lay me down to sleep" prayer. No, it was heart- wrenching and honest, selfless and humble, more a prayer asking for forgiveness than a prayer asking "the Santa Claus God" for things, healing, or a nice life. Nehemiah acknowledged the God of Heaven as great and awesome in an honest way, not manipulating Him to hand over the goods and then everything will be just fine. It was a mature, yet childlike prayer confessing God's never-failing promise to keep His Word to always love us.[10]

Then the clincher.

This was a prayer that separates winners from whiners. He says to the most powerful being in the universe, "I'm sorry. I am sorry, I have screwed up, I have messed up so badly that I do not deserve to even speak to You! Yes, even my family and I have let You down. We squandered what You have given to us." And God heard his prayer.

You too may be able to identify with such heartache and pain, but the voice of logic says things have to get better. Just do what you're doing, or transfer this balance to that card, or perhaps a friend suggests refinancing one more time or investing in this stock or property. But you know deep down inside that the life you are living is a living hell—a life without hope, a charade.

The hours locked in a cell seemed like days. I had time I never wanted to ponder the life I had embraced. The life that had brought me so low that now I was in jail. These devastating choices I made kept replaying in my mind as I was living a life that did not satisfy. The money, the pleasures, the consumption—all were empty. They just could not satisfy my appetite for more. I remember one evening months before I was arrested where I spent over a thousand dollars at a restaurant only to wake up the next day wishing the night before had been a nightmare. It *was* a nightmare, but it had happened. I was a kid who grew up in a Christian home, going to Christian schools, and learning Christian things, but what I was missing I had substituted with the things of this world. What I should have bought was the truth. Solomon said, "Buy the truth and do not sell it …"[11]

If you have gotten this far in this book, God wants to speak to your heart and you feel it. Take a moment and get quiet with the God of the universe who owns it all, including you, and pray the prayer of Nehemiah. [12]

DAY 5

Selfish or Selfless?

" ... LET YOUR EAR BE ATTENTIVE AND YOUR EYES OPEN TO HEAR THE
PRAYER YOUR SERVANT IS PRAYING BEFORE YOU DAY AND NIGHT FOR
YOUR SERVANTS ... ." (NEHEMIAH 1:6)

"WE REGARD GOD AS AN AIRMAN REGARDS HIS PARACHUTE; IT'S THERE
FOR EMERGENCIES, BUT HE HOPES HE'LL NEVER HAVE TO USE IT."
– C.S. LEWIS

"A BANK IS A PLACE THAT WILL LEND YOU MONEY IF YOU CAN PROVE
THAT YOU DON'T NEED IT." – BOB HOPE

Nehemiah then does something truly extraordinary. Actually, he does something so radical that this is where we usually have a disconnect with Nehemiah and start to ask, "Who does this guy think he is?" Or worse, as one out of the twelve commentaries studied in regard to the life and times of Nehemiah, "He has got to be a fake!"[13] Nehemiah begged God to listen to his prayer to save his people and to bring them back together to the place God had chosen as the place for Him and His people to live.[14] It was not a prayer of, "Save me, God, and I am sure You will take care of the others; but my needs are most important," but the paradigm-changing plea to ask God to intervene on someone else's behalf. This prayer changed Nehemiah forever. This communication with the God of the universe brought him from material comfort to great gain, and he chose to invest his life into the lives of others.

He had no idea what such a prayer would bring, or what he would do about it, but he knew he was going to do everything in his power to right a great wrong. He was one man with only a prayer to save an entire people and their city. One day he was enjoying the markings of success; the next day he had a complete and radical heart and life change.

It reminds me of the movie *Jerry Maguire*, in which the main character is a high-powered sports agent and attorney who has single-handedly driven up the prices of the talent he represents by hard negotiating tactics that leave families, friends, and the health of his clients way behind. He is rich, successful in the world's eyes, and his life is enviable. Until that one night—the night when he visited a pro-hockey-player client who was just regaining consciousness in the hospital after yet another concussion. In a partial catatonic state the player couldn't remember where he was or who the people in his room were, but recognized his agent, Jerry Maguire. "This is my agent and I have got to get the bonus. I get a bonus for playing all my games." The player's son, who was thirteen-years-old, walked Jerry out of the hospital room and pleaded with him, saying his dad had three concussions that season and he could not hold out much longer, only to hear Jerry Maguire say, "Nothing can stop your dad … ." The boy was utterly dejected as he feared for his dad's life. Later that evening Jerry Maguire had a nightmare and woke with a new conscience, and wrote a new mission statement, one that put people ahead of profits. He distributed it to everyone in the company, and he was promptly fired as a result. That would be the typical, good-guys-finish-last, defeatist scenario. In Hollywood–style, however, there is a girl who believes in him and, against all odds, the two of them rise back to the top by putting people before profits.

We know just how to pray during times of misfortune for ourselves. But when it is not directly affecting us or ours, we thank God that we are still intact and healthy and blessed. But when we beg God on behalf of others, we are tapping into the heart of God. The problem is, however, that it seems that we just don't get the answers to our prayers in the financial realm. The reason? Because we so often ask with the wrong motives. Nehemiah's motives were pure, as he knew he was interceding for people that were hurting, and he wanted to help. The disciple James said, "… You do not have, because you do not ask God. When you ask you do not receive, because you ask with wrong motives, that you may spend what you get on your pleasures."[15]

After eight days in this prison-style jail and unable to raise the million-dollar bail, miraculously, it was reduced and I was able to get out via a bail bondsman. When they announced my release, it was no great thrill or relief. Days earlier I had prayed every moment to be released and then I invited this God, whom I called my "Savior," into a friendship. My heart was already released. I took the next hour going cell to cell telling the inmates about my newfound freedom in something deeper than jailhouse religion. It was a freedom with a deep heart-satisfying, stress-calming, anxiety-freeing, peace-giving that had eluded me until then. My new wise advice to the fellow prisoners and those whom Jesus Christ loved deeply was: "Don't lose hope, this could be the most peaceful time of your life"—and yours too!

DAY 6

A New Hope

"WE HAVE ACTED VERY WICKEDLY TOWARD YOU. WE HAVE NOT OBEYED THE COMMANDS, DECREES AND LAWS YOU GAVE … ." (NEHEMIAH 1:7)

"MONEY IS BETTER THAN POVERTY, IF ONLY FOR FINANCIAL REASONS."
– WOODY ALLEN

"[GOD] IS NOT PROUD … HE WILL HAVE US EVEN THOUGH WE HAVE SHOWN THAT WE PREFER EVERYTHING ELSE TO HIM." – C.S. LEWIS

Who in this century will forget the original *Star Wars* movie entitled *The New Hope,* where a young Luke Skywalker was destined to save the galaxy from the evil dark side led by the ruthless Darth Vader? It was the classic good-against-evil theme and we all had to wait fourteen years to find out which side would win in this cosmic action adventure movie. But Nehemiah faced a real threat that wasn't storyboarded by genius writers, directors, and special-effects experts. He was Esther's male counterpart, thirty years later, to save the Jews again—as well as the city this time.

Nehemiah tapped into the source of hope for him and his people. He knew this was the time and place he had been born for—his divine destiny. He was to be used in a powerful way to bring his people healing, no matter how in debt, scattered, in pain, or hopeless they were. He was chosen for this moment. You can say with certainty that Nehemiah was raised to a royal position for such a time as this.[16]

God is the source of all hope. He is not *a* source of hope. Most people live a lifetime without truly understanding the difference. We place our hope in money, or what money might buy, or people, or love, or our own strength, or a thousand other things. But what if there was a certain center of hope? A source of all hope, once tapped into, produced complete joy and peace; what if that were possible? What would you give for that type of confidence? What would you risk for a life that could possess this total satisfaction? Was Thoreau's statement in the opening chapter of *Walden* correct when he said, "The mass of men lead lives of quiet desperation"? [17]

When we view God as an option of hope instead of the only source of hope, our lives will resound the real truth in Thoreau's words written over 150 years ago. The question is not, "Is there a hope?" or "Is there a God?" Rather, when will we acknowledge the God of the universe who intimately knows us and wants us to have a life that is full of joy? We do not want to arrive at the end of our lives admitting that what we pursued and what we invested in reduced us to a mass of men leading lives of quiet, or as in our society, very vocal desperation. As we saw with great transparency in the life of Nehemiah in Day 1, we must surrender to the God who made us and who bought us with his blood sacrifice on the cross, nearly 2000 years ago. [18]

I was released from jail, but the trial was pending. I did not know what the future held, nor did I have the foggiest idea that I would have to leave law school, take a felony conviction to avoid jail time, pay back the money I stole, plus tens of thousands of dollars I stupidly borrowed (from credit cards, personal loans, and student loans), get dumped by my girl, and even get denied employment at Pizza Hut as a delivery boy. The great hope I had when I was released on bail crashed and burned when faced with the reality of my future.

The kid who used to joke and brag, "My future looks so bright I have to wear shades," only a few months later was living in his car under the I-95 exit ramp, courtesy of the assistant manager of the valet parking concession at the Hyatt Regency. Hopeless, once again.

Just like Peter when he stepped out of the boat, the waves had become my focus, and not the Savior. I was fortunate to get a job as a valet parker at the Hyatt Regency in downtown Miami, but I did not have one part of the uniform that was necessary to keep the job: black sneakers.

To add insult to injury, the only shoes on the market that were approved by the hotel were all-black Reeboks, which retailed for fifty dollars. That might as well have been a million dollars to a kid who was working for food. I did not give up though. I went into a McCrory's Drug Store and purchased a pair of ladies' garden shoes at a cost of $5.99.

There were no shoes for someone like me in that price range. I didn't care. My pride had been shattered and now my basic needs were more important. The shoes were black with a white band around the outside. The supervisor at the valet parking facility told me I had to go home because my uniform was not adequate since my shoes were not all black.

I was hungry and devastated, but I was very aware that my day job, which provided for the minimum payments on most of my debts, was within walking distance. I carried a black Magic Marker and colored the sides of both shoes. I kept the marker with me as I ran because the color wore off with nearly every stride.

I always waited patiently on the ramp to be in position for the next car that drove up to this posh hotel. The gleaming chrome and multiple-baked enamel sports cars and luxury sedans made their way up and the local celebrities exited their vehicles.

My turn came and the car was a new Jaguar. The man who eased out was TV news anchorman and local celebrity, Dwight Lauderdale. I was pleased to be his driver. With a quick look and a nod, I jumped in the Jag and looked for the key. This was my first time in such a luxury car, even though I had lived a lie for nearly a year before an anonymous tip opened up the biggest embezzlement conspiracy in the area's law enforcement's history.

I found the key and turned on the wildcat. Unfortunately, for me, the car was already running. I was horrified when the engine squealed as if on the verge of total combustion. If looks could kill, I would not have survived. All I could do was put the car in drive before I was physically removed from the injured kitty.

I was hopeless once again. I was broke, wearing ladies' garden shoes, hungry, my financial dreams dead and gone, and now I couldn't even operate a car. I was at the bottom. I was bankrupt and the hope that I had felt in jail was fleeing quickly.

I turned on the radio looking for God. I found a Christian radio station in Miami and heard the voice of Larry Burkett. He was talking about how God owned it all, and how we are stewards or managers of what He has entrusted to us. He said that most of us have been poor managers and deserve the punishment of our actions, but there is hope and forgiveness. He then described how great and loving, longsuffering and rich our God is and that He cannot wait to pick us up and dust us off and show us that we can trust in Him.

I realized for the first time that I was embezzling God's possessions too. I should have been fired, but for His incredible love I lived to see another day and had yet another chance. I asked God to forgive the way I had mismanaged and mishandled His treasury, and to give me another chance to show Him I could be trusted.

From that night, my spending habits and my heart were changed forever. By radically altering my lifestyle over the next four years, I was able to pay back the money I stole, incur no more debt, and start using money God's way. I eventually became a CPA and a financial counselor, even working with Larry Burkett's Crown Financial Ministries.

No matter where you are right now, if no one will give you a chance to be trusted, God will. He trusted me, and my life changed as a testimony to His unfailing grace.

DAY 7

Serious Soul Searching

" ... IF YOU ARE UNFAITHFUL, I WILL SCATTER YOU ... ." (NEHEMIAH 1:8)

"FEAR CAN KEEP US UP ALL NIGHT LONG, BUT FAITH MAKES
ONE FINE PILLOW." – PHILLIP GULLEY

"MONEY IS NOT THE MOST IMPORTANT THING IN THE WORLD. LOVE IS.
FORTUNATELY, I LOVE MONEY." – JACKIE MASON

While Nehemiah speaks to God for many days, he reminisces once again and asks God to remember the Law He spoke to Moses. God's promise was that if they were unfaithful, He would scatter them, but if they returned to the loving and compassionate living God, and obeyed His commands, He would do something so incredible that it would seem almost miraculous.[19] He would gather all the people, even the ones held prisoner in the most remote parts of the Earth, to a place God had chosen for them. Nehemiah believed God, and his faith was being strengthened.

Today your faith needs a similar strengthening. Money is just a test of our faith. As we remember God's promises, see how He has kept them and that, as we obey Him, we find there are certain blessings that just cannot be attained any other way. Bob Coy, the pastor of Calvary Chapel, a mega-church in Fort Lauderdale, Florida, has summed it up this way: "God cannot bless unblessable behavior." We have a hard time with that because we say, "If God loves everyone, then He really shouldn't withhold anything good from us." But this is what God's Word says about that faulty belief: "No good thing does he withhold from those whose walk is blameless." Yes, we can receive great comfort in that promise from the only One who has kept all the promises He has made, but we cannot walk blameless while we are not living an obedient life.

Perhaps this is where you find yourself. Struggling to make ends meet, more month then money. A budget is a foreign language, your marriage is in shambles or getting there. Perhaps you are now unmarried, and contemplating bankruptcy, and you wish you could just win the lottery so your wildest dreams would come true—which are far less lofty than they used to be. That is the lie people have been living and believing their entire lives. Now all you want out of your financial life is a little peace and no more debt, and hope for the years to come. God has a plan and it means believing what God says about money, and then obeying Him.

Most of the 2,350 verses in the Bible on money and possessions are warnings against the mishandling of God's resources. When we do not follow His way, we are absolutely, unequivocally going to feel pain. And if you have never experienced financial pain, ask anyone who has (essentially anyone who breathes), how it feels and they will tell you it is the worst gut-wrenching, future-zapping, relationship-ending, tear-producing, heart-tearing, energy-sapping pain you have ever experienced. Some prefer death to this very real and avoidable self-inflicted pain.

Now it is time to follow the One who is not trying to take your fun and excitement away. He is the One who is trying to give you the life that is *truly* life. If you think the pain of following your own path is not so bad, perhaps you need a bit more pain until you are ready to do it God's way.

The source of our sorrow or trouble in our finances is not from God, because if we do it His way, He promises to "add no sorrow to it." But since the evil one does not want us to live a financial life without the sorrow, he continues to deceive us into thinking we know better. And why not? We are smart,

23

educated, well read, and have many people who will tell us that what we are doing is according to Hoyle. We have been deceived into thinking that obeying God will require us to give all of our money away and we will consequently have nothing. So obviously we cannot use God's Word as a textbook for living. As a result, many will never experience the incredible joy and peace He has in store for us.

DAY 8

Admire, Desire, Require, Acquire

"... BUT IF YOU RETURN TO ME ... I WILL GATHER THEM FROM THERE AND BRING THEM TO THE PLACE I HAVE CHOSEN ... ." (NEHEMIAH 1:9).

"IF YOU GIVE UP A THING OUT OF A STERN SENSE OF DUTY, YOU WOULD CONTINUE TO WANT IT BACK, AND THAT UNSATISFIED DESIRE WILL MAKE TROUBLE FOR YOU. ONLY GIVE UP A THING WHEN YOU WANT SOME OTHER CONDITION SO MUCH THAT THE THING NO LONGER HAS ANY ATTRACTION FOR YOU, OR WHEN IT SEEMS TO INTERFERE WITH THAT WHICH IS MORE GREATLY DESIRED." – GANDHI

In massive black lettering, a newly affixed, eye-catching message over the multi-million- dollar renovation at a local mall in South Florida speaks to the real heart of worship by proclaiming, "Admire, Desire, Require, Acquire—All Within the Realm of Possibility." The message is not subtle. I see something, feast my eyes on it, desire it in my heart, and this inanimate object becomes my singular focus. The object may take on an almost mythical expectation in our minds—an expectation that no earthly object can fulfill. Or, as George Bernard Shaw put it: "There are two tragedies in life. One is to lose your heart's desire. The other is to gain it." When was the last time an object of desire truly satiated?

Once you have affixed your desire, nothing will stand in your way of procuring it, regardless of your means to pay for it. This is the heart of the worship of things and getting more things; those things we don't have but will soon discover we require for our very existence to be complete. We wonder why our lives

25

lack authentic satisfaction while we are looking for significance from things. The question is not a new one. For centuries we have been seeking the source of satisfaction. The Greek Stoic philosopher Epictetus touched on the futility of indulgence and retreated: "Freedom is not procured by a full enjoyment of what is desired, but by controlling the desire."

The answer lies in focusing our desire on the richest and most satisfying treasure—Jesus Christ.

We are submerged in a listless cycle of self-satisfaction and it is time to ask ourselves, "Whom will I serve?" It is not a trick question, nor a rhetorical question. It is a question that we must ask ourselves daily.

About eight hundred years before Nehemiah, when God brought the Israelites out of Egypt with their reluctant leader Moses and his brother to speak for him, their rebellion caused them to wander for forty years in the wilderness until Joshua would lead them into the Promised Land.[20]

The rebellious Israelites continued to turn their eyes from God and worship idols. Before Joshua passed on to be with the Lord, he challenged the people one last time in much the same way his predecessor Moses did. He gathered the leaders, the judges, the wise, the noble, the Bible teachers, and the pastors [21] to give them this final counsel from the heart, "Now fear the Lord and serve him with all faithfulness. Throw away the gods your forefathers worshiped … and serve the Lord" (Joshua 24:14). It's a typical pep talk to those of us who "just wanna have fun" and enjoy life without hurting anyone else. But the god of materialism and pleasure is a fickle master.

Deep down inside we think that if we truly follow Him, we will not be able to drive a new car or buy a nice home or eat at our favorite restaurant. We are doomed to a mind-numbing existence of boredom, shuffling through life with our heads hung low until we reach Heaven. This falsehood has consumed more Christians and repelled more folks from becoming Christians than any other single deception.

We have got it backwards. The life that is truly life is one that is fully engaged in the adventure dreamed up by the Creator of the universe for each of us. It is only then that we will fully come alive. It is only then that we will be fully satisfied. It is not that our desires are too great for God; it is that they are too small.

As the great Christian thinker C.S. Lewis said in his book, *Weight of Glory*, "If we consider the unblushing promises of reward and the staggering nature of the rewards promised in the Gospels, it would seem that Our Lord finds our desire not too strong, but too weak. We are half-hearted creatures, fooling about with drink and sex and ambition when infinite joy is offered us. We are like ignorant children who want to continue making mud pies in a slum because we cannot imagine what is meant by the offer of a vacation at the sea. We are far too easily pleased."

We must upgrade our desires, not pray that God takes them away so we can be good little Christians or nice guys or the man or woman my church wants me to be. No, God made us for much more then simply acquiring more stuff. The truth is that you will only find satisfaction in Him, and He promises to satisfy your desires with good things, not temporarily, but for a lifetime.[22]

Remember Joshua's pep talk to the important people? He said something truly cutting edge. "But if serving the Lord seems undesirable to you, then choose for yourselves this day whom you will serve ..." (Joshua 24:15). Did I hear that correctly? Did Joshua just say *if* serving God is not your cup of tea, don't do it? Is he crazy? Doesn't he know that he could get in serious trouble for saying something like that? God is going to have some serious "Clean up on Aisle 5" for this slip of the tongue. Joshua must be getting senile. He is 110 years old, you know.

Joshua continued his final speech by saying you could choose the gods your relatives worshiped in the desert. Or even better, the gods of the land you are living in, the wicked people who have been trying to kill you for many years now. Joshua said,

"… but as for me and my household, we will serve the Lord." [23] You can imagine the response, shaming the people like that. The Scriptures say that the people answered with the same heated plea, "Far be it from us to forsake the Lord to serve other gods!" They went on to say that it was the Lord God who brought them up out of slavery and performed incredible miracles and protected them, and drove out all of the bad guys from the places they traveled. Then they said to Joshua, "We too will serve the Lord, because he is our God." [24]

You have got to choose today whether you want hope, joy, and peace, or heartache, frustration, anxiety, fear, anger, greed, and the rest of the usual suspects you have been harboring. No more safe passage; tell them to come out with their hands up, and upgrade your life. Jesus Christ is the *only* source of hope and He wants to fill you with all joy and peace, not just a fix to get you by until you buy something else that temporarily satisfies. No, He wants to fill you with *all joy and peace*.

But there is a catch. He wants us to trust Him. Plain and simple. No cartwheels, no somersaults, no hot-coal walking, but plain and simple trust. And here is His entire modus operandi all wrapped up in one life-giving, life-changing verse that has the power to bring every person who has accepted Christ as their Savior complete joy and peace: "May the God of hope fill you with all joy and peace as you trust in him, so that you may overflow with hope by the power of the Holy Spirit" (Romans 15:13).

When we take this step away from the gods of this world– the spending god, the credit god, the god of things, the god of pleasure or what money can buy– we are saying to God, "I am yours and I trust You." John Piper, the pastor of Bethlehem Baptist Church in Minneapolis, Minnesota, in his book, *Don't Waste Your Life,* says, "It was not always plain to me that pursuing God's glory would be virtually the same as pursuing my joy. Now I see that millions of people waste their lives because they think these paths are two and not one."

So trust in God, accept the unforced rhythms of His grace, and reap the supreme peace and joy the world cannot provide.

DAY 9

Give Me Success!

"GIVE YOUR SERVANT SUCCESS TODAY BY GRANTING HIM FAVOR IN THE PRESENCE OF THIS MAN." (NEHEMIAH 1:11B)

"TRY NOT TO BECOME A MAN OF SUCCESS, BUT RATHER TRY TO BECOME A MAN OF VALUE." – ALBERT EINSTEIN

"SO YOU THINK THAT MONEY IS THE ROOT OF ALL EVIL. HAVE YOU EVER ASKED WHAT IS THE ROOT OF ALL MONEY?" – AYN RAND

Nehemiah begged God through repeated prayers that He would have success—a selfish prayer at first glance. It is a startling window into Nehemiah's soul. Could he really pray continuously for success?

How do you pray? Using my paraphrase, this is the whole of Nehemiah's continuous prayer. See if it resembles yours: "Lord, please hear my prayer, I am your servant, and hear the prayers of my family, who are your servants also; we love, respect, and want to live for you. Would you give me success today in the presence of the king, my boss?"[25]

You see, his biggest obstacle was a good job with an impossible boss. They did not share the same faith and their backgrounds couldn't have been more opposite. Nehemiah was Jewish, and King Artaxerxes was Persian, a descendant of Ishmael. They were known to hate the Jews. Yet Nehemiah was perhaps the highest and most trusted person in the palace.

He could not possibly mess up this great job. This was the job of the century and he was about to ask for time off to help rebuild his city. Nehemiah decided *safe* was no longer an option.

He knew that giving in to the attraction of the worthless things of life was the same as clinging to the worthless idols of the evil people in Babylon. As a result, he would forfeit the truly satisfying gift of the life that is truly life.

The Prophet Jonah had been offered the opportunity for greatness also and he ran the other way. God didn't want him to miss this incredible journey to see massive life change, though. These were his words as he thought he was going die in the belly of a great fish: "Those who cling to worthless idols forfeit the grace that could be theirs" (Jonah 2:8). God had the fish spit him up after three days and Jonah followed the path that God had for him. He went to the wicked country to tell the people there about the love of God and they all turned their hearts from evil and followed Him. Hundreds of thousands of people were saved, all in one crusade! That is more than even Billy Graham has accomplished in one event, and Jonah had only one line to communicate to the people of Nineveh. That was an awesome display of God's power and Jonah's heart was changed in the process, too.

You too may face a similar situation at your job, with your house, or in life in general and it just is not the time to take that heroic leap of faith. You may be telling yourself, "Maybe Nehemiah could do it, but he did not have my situation and my responsibility." Or you may be reluctant because you are still not sure you have a mission like Nehemiah. You would truly love to get your financial life back on track or straightened out for the first time and do it God's way. You believe He does have a good plan for you, but may think, "I just can't do this _____ _____" (you fill in the blank). You *can* do it. Take this next step and know He will give you success because this endeavor is from God. God wants you to have His idea of success.

God wants you to upgrade your fear to grace. Grace is simply getting something you have not earned. It is a gift and only God can deliver. What will it be today: fear or grace?

You will not be satisfied with prayers for the world's definition of success. You know the prayer: "Lord, may I be rich or have this dream home I have always longed for so I can have Bible studies with the neighbors. Wayward travelers can rest there in one of the extra bedrooms, and we can form a local chapter of "Big Houses for Christ" (BHFC for short) and many people will hear the Word of the Lord and their hearts will be changed because of my big house." Or maybe your hope from God is the job that pays more or is more comfortable; or perhaps it is your car that is giving you anxiety and the only thing that can release you from that prison is a Hummer so you can drive for the Lord. Or the vacation home you need so you can let others stay there and you can travel for the Lord, too ... We may have good intentions but we have been deceived because somewhere, sometime, we were led to believe that this is where success is found, and where success is found is where I will find joy and peace.

It is time to upgrade to God's awesome plan for your life, where only lasting joy and peace lie. Come drink at this fountain. This truth is so perfectly memorialized for us through the ancient psalm of Asaph. It is something to hold onto and remember during times of the evil one's schemes: " ... open wide your mouth and I will fill it."[26] Are you ready to ask for God's idea of success and upgrade yours?

DAY 10

Fear Factor

"I WAS VERY MUCH AFRAID, BUT I SAID TO THE KING ... ."
(NEHEMIAH 2:2B-3A)

"TAKE THE FIRST STEP IN FAITH. YOU DON'T HAVE TO SEE THE WHOLE
STAIRCASE, JUST TAKE THE FIRST STEP." – MARTIN LUTHER KING, JR.

"MONEY NEVER MADE A MAN HAPPY YET, NOR WILL IT. THE MORE A
MAN HAS, THE MORE HE WANTS. INSTEAD OF FILLING A VACUUM,
IT MAKES ONE." – BEN FRANKLIN

Upon hearing of the seemingly insurmountable task that would be his charge, Nehemiah wept. Now, this is not something you see a man do very often, especially one with Nehemiah's power. Don't confuse his vulnerability with weakness. He was a real man about to face a hopeless and very real situation, humanly speaking. He was going to ask the king to grant him a leave of absence for an indefinite amount of time and to give him letters for materials and safety. [27]

Imagine going to your boss with these requests. You would labor over every word for days, painstakingly working up the courage to breach the subject. You would probably imagine an entire dialog, filling in your boss's responses: "I really wish I could, but ...", or "I really want to, believe me, but budget constraints prevent me from doing it. I am sure you understand." Or if you are an optimist, "You're a valued member of the team and a sharp dresser to boot, but the answer is still 'no.'"

Nehemiah walked into the throne room, head in hands, shaking, physically sick. He took the wine, tasted it with his quivering lips, and brought it over to the king. With his gaze fixed on the floor, shoulders drooping, Nehemiah opened his mouth and raised his sweaty palms toward the king to plead for his people.

You can probably relate to Nehemiah's demeanor. Just when you thought it couldn't get worse, it did. Interest, penalties, late charges, car payments, day care, the IRS wants more, sneakers are more expensive this year than last, and let's not even talk about gas prices. Is there hope? Or have you already raised the white flag in surrender, not to God, but to debt, and the irrefutable fact that you will never, ever, be out of it. You will never buy a car with cash, not even a clunker. At this rate you will have to sell your house for much less than it is worth just to barely get out of debt, and, to add insult to injury, you will never have enough to retire. As a matter of fact, you are worth more dead than alive. You have received your death sentence and all you can do is resign yourself to it.

I could go on with Satan's lies, but you have heard them often enough and do not need to hear them from me. The God of hope is so much bigger than any economic system and He's waiting patiently for you to hold out your hand, take His, and walk through that dark room. This is where miracles are born. Not the scenario where we have no financial worries, a hundred grand in the bank, and a posh retirement. No, there is no trusting God in that situation.

When we face impossible odds that even a first grader with ADD could focus on long enough to tell you to run, you know it's bad, and you need a Savior. That is where faith comes in—being absolutely sure of what we hope for and absolutely certain of what we don't see. This same faith that enables mere mortals to do great things can only come from God and it shines out every time ordinary people follow Him through impossible situations, much like the one you are facing right now.

Nehemiah knew the odds, but faced his giant. He knew God wanted him to be the person to save a city, but facing his boss seemed too difficult. Despite his fear he stepped forward and God used him, even in his anxious state, just like God is going to use you even though you are fearful. Though it may be hard to see sometimes, God is bigger than any king, principality, or power. He is bigger than the real estate market, bigger than the IRS, bigger than the stock market. It is only when we realize how small and insignificant the powers of this world are that we can face them without trepidation. C.S. Lewis recognized this: "If you read history you will find that the Christians who did most for the present world were precisely those who thought most of the next. It is since Christians have largely ceased to think of the other world that they have become so ineffective in this."

What is it you want? Are you afraid to ask at this point because your situation is totally different from Nehemiah's? Yours is self-inflicted and as a result you could never ask God to help, to intervene, to move in the heart of your boss or your creditor or your landlord. We just don't deserve it. None of us do. It is time now to upgrade. It is a crazy, lopsided deal He is offering. He gets all the praise and glory and we get all of the joy and peace. Let's accept it.

DAY 11

Rescuing God

This may have been Nehemiah's finest moment. He was completely vulnerable to the king. He was wearing his heart on his sleeve. His face told the complete story of his anguish and the uncertainty of the future.

This is the time we usually lean on our own intellect and attempt to control the situation.[28] After all, Nehemiah was dealing with someone who certainly would not and could not empathize with him. What he was about to request was way outside the lines, far beyond his employment contract, and not a very good strategy when communicating with a boss. Humanly speaking, this was the time to negotiate a package that would be a win-win situation for both parties.

So this is the time to candy-coat the message to the king, right? Tell him what he wants to hear, make the request in a compelling way, and be ready to overcome any objection.

But that is not what Nehemiah did. Nehemiah chose to level with the king, risking the worst possible outcome. He obeyed God and left the consequences to Him.

Rescuing God is all about making something happen yourself because you don't think God is big enough to do it. You become the gatekeeper of God's plans, His eyes and ears on the ground. Nehemiah didn't try to rescue God, he simply communicated what God had placed on his heart and was willing to do whatever the king permitted him to do.

There are great reasons to take matters into your own hands because some things are too important to leave to God. What if He blows it?

Nehemiah knew all men's hearts were in God's hands, and that he could trust Him. He knew God withholds nothing from those who walk blamelessly.[29]

Will you rescue God this time? Or will you let Him rescue you? If there is more month than money, will you charge your groceries—that *is* why God gave you great credit, isn't it? Then God can send you a check to pay off the credit card, right?

This can also mean taking matters into your own hands and not quite revealing all of the truth, as the truth may hurt your situation. I can remember a one-on-one coaching appointment with a gentleman who, after hearing God's Word, revealed that he had added hours that he had not worked to his paycheck and was paid more than he had honestly earned. He was moved to come clean and wanted to do the right thing, but his mind said, "Make it up on the next payroll and lower the earnings by the amount dishonestly taken." This would smooth out the situation and all would be made right. But the employer would never know a theft had occurred. Is this merely situational ethics? No. The road less traveled is obeying God and leaving the consequences to Him.

He humbly went to his employer and asked for forgiveness with the stolen money in hand, along with 20 percent more and an "I'm sorry." The employer was absolutely blown away by his employee's honesty, as no one had ever come to him and confessed such a situation. He commended the employee and gave him more responsibility since he knew he could be trusted.

Stop leaning on your own understanding. Trust God and stop rescuing Him. He doesn't need our help.

DAY 12

If It Pleases the King

"THEN I PRAYED TO THE GOD OF HEAVEN, AND I ANSWERED THE KING, 'IF IT PLEASES THE KING AND IF YOUR SERVANT HAS FOUND FAVOR IN HIS SIGHT ... .'" (NEHEMIAH 2:4B-5A)

"IF GOD IS IN CONTROL, WHY IS MY LIFE SUCH A MESS?"
– MICHAEL YOUSSEF

"MONEY OFTEN COSTS TOO MUCH." – EMERSON

God was in control of the plan and Nehemiah became part of it. All the success would be God's and all the joy and peace would be Nehemiah's. What an incredible God! We certainly do not deserve such an awesome arrangement. Especially when we are merely God's pawns in the great miracles and events He has in store for us.

But that is the story of the God who loves you more than life itself, as He has proved by laying down His life for us. There is no greater love than someone who lays down his life for his friends. He calls us friends and proves it every day.[30]

When asked by the most powerful human king on earth at the time, "What is it you want?" Nehemiah quickly uttered another prayer to his heavenly King.[31]

"If it please the king, then allow me to go."[32] God had already moved in the heart of the king because he granted Nehemiah's request for a lengthy leave of absence.

Our part is to respond to God's leading, seek His wisdom through prayer, and devour His written Word.[33] God does all the heavy lifting. We just need to show up and do what He asks us to do. If we understand and follow this way of life, we are guaranteed a life that is truly life with all the joy and peace that comes with it.[34]

The question we must ask now is, "Is the way I use His money pleasing to Him?"

It took four months to approach the king and ask for permission to go on a mission from God. It would take less time to rebuild the wall.

DAY 13

God Is Not Looking for a Hero; He *Is* the Hero

"And because the gracious hand of my God was upon me,
the king granted my requests." (Nehemiah 2:8b)

"Being a hero is about the shortest-lived profession on earth."
– Will Rogers

"If you want to see what God thinks of money, just look at
all the people He gave it to." – Dorothy Parker

When we get our arms around this truth we can better understand and accept the absolute awesome adventure He has set out before us. You see He is not waiting for us to come into our own and become the hero of the world. That would make us and our decisions, accomplishments, and our lives the center of the universe. He is the center of the universe and He beckons us to come follow Him and join Him for the only soul-satisfying adventure on the planet. This is not bad news for us. It is incredible, liberating news because we know deep down inside that we do not have all the answers and ability, and we really don't always have the best motives, since we are still human. We can also be vulnerable if given the right situation.

God makes an astounding offer to follow Him, and let Him use our gifts and talents, the things we enjoy, and the way we are wired. He will make a powerful combination from all that which will be used to touch people's lives with the truth of His love. You see, most people treat God like meeting the pastor at the mall. A cordial, "Hello, pastor, nice to see you. How are you doing? Nice sermon the other day" (although we don't really remember it all that much). That's the respect we show. In Jesus' day we would have shown similar respect for a person by calling him "Master." The English word is translated from the Greek word *epistat s,* which means any sort of superintendent or overseer. Much like us, when the professional fisherman of Jesus' day, Simon Peter, was asked by Jesus Christ to use his fishing boat as a makeshift stage to speak to the crowd of people on the shore, he obliged the Rabbi. [35] After all, people were watching and he didn't want to insult anyone. It could be bad for business. But when the Rabbi said, "Let's fish," our Peter must have thought, "This guy ought to stick with his knitting. Pastor, you do the preaching and I'll do the fishing, and if you ever want to know anything about what I do, go ahead and ask. I will give you quite an education." But being the professional fisherman Peter said, "Master, we have worked hard all night and haven't caught anything." At this point there was probably a pregnant pause before he obliged the Pastor and said, "But because you say so, I will let down the nets."

I can certainly relate to Peter here. Have you ever had some credible person tell you to do something you knew didn't make sense, but you did it anyway and you were right? There are many who give unsolicited advice, the proverbial "two-cents worth," and often we are expected to take heed, only to prove them wrong. Sometimes it is at our expense. This has scarred us from both listening to wise counsel and, more critically, following God.

Fortunately, our fisherman chose the right path. As soon as he obeyed this Pastor, he caught such a large amount of fish his nets began to break. Then he signaled for his buddies and they all caught so many fish that the boats began to sink. You understand that the reason they caught that many fish was only because Peter obeyed. It wasn't because Peter was the hero. No, he was now part of massive life change, including his own. As soon as this seasoned, salty-dog fisherman, who had seen it all, saw something so outrageous, so beyond his wildest dreams, so miraculous, he was moved. His heart got it. It wasn't about Peter. It was about the God of the galaxy who was speaking and standing next to a rugged man's man, a real man who fished all night sometimes, who smelt like smelt, who probably had a net-mending kit in his pocket, and a permanent tan. This man was now in the company of the Son of God. When Peter saw this happening, he fell at Jesus' knees and said, "Go away from me, Lord; I am a sinful man!" [36] Then the Savior of the world spoke these words to him, "Don't be afraid." Your Father spoke these words a long time ago to you and me also.

Nehemiah must have thought, "Who am I? I am essentially a prisoner here in the palace; granted, a very highly compensated one at that, and I can come and go as I like, but I can't be the person who leads an entire nation back to their historic city and rebuild it too! God, I am not that hero." God's response was, as He spoke to Peter that day on the fishing boat, "Don't be afraid; from now on you will catch men." Only at this point does a real man stand or fall. You see, all of the miracles, all of the evidence of a Savior, all of the trials He brings you through culminate in this defining moment. Peter was smitten by someone who was able to pierce his soul with His eyes. He could not look at Him and ask Him to go, to leave, by saying, "I am not worthy." This time he wasn't just hearing the words of the Pastor. No, this time he heard the words of the One who breathed life into the nostrils of Adam, and everyone born since then. When the world's greatest treasure asks you to follow Him, and you have seen His power filtered through His love, you cannot respond in any other way. Peter pulled his boat to shore, left his fishing tackle, nets, bait, poles, gaffs, life jackets, and followed Him. Nehemiah did likewise, almost 500 years earlier. He left the comfort of the palace to do something I am sure he wondered how he was going to pull off. But he knew he could trust the One who had led him to this defining moment in life.

You are at a similar crossroad. You can either stay safe, comfortable, and longing for more; or you can trust God, our hero, and follow Him for the most satisfying adventure ever. You may be asking the question, "What does this have to do with my finances?" The answer? Everything. Unless you understand the basic truths of ownership, how can you do as Nehemiah or Peter or many others have done, and leave the comforts of the mediocre for a truly satisfying life? Until you have the penetrating experience of God speaking to your heart, you will continue to think of God as merely a superintendent and not your absolutely infallible, loving-to-the-death God. You are going to be stalled right where you are until that moment. Why not today choose to follow Him?

DAY 14

Strategic Tools for the Mission

"... MAY I HAVE LETTERS TO THE GOVERNORS OF TRANS-EUPHRATES, SO THAT THEY WILL PROVIDE ME SAFE-CONDUCT UNTIL I ARRIVE IN JUDAH? AND MAY I HAVE A LETTER TO ASAPH ... SO HE WILL GIVE ME TIMBER TO MAKE BEAMS FOR THE GATES ...?" (NEHEMIAH 2:7-8)

"MAKE ALL YOU CAN, SAVE ALL YOU CAN, GIVE ALL YOU CAN."
– JOHN WESLEY

"DON'T TELL ME WHERE YOUR PRIORITIES ARE. SHOW ME WHERE YOU SPEND YOUR MONEY AND I'LL TELL YOU WHAT THEY ARE."
– JAMES FRICK

Financially, you are motivated to get going, to jump into the how-to's, the nuts and bolts, and see the progress. But before that we have to unpack the financial stuff that will delay our progress and pack up the tools that will get us closer to the goal of building our financial fortress.

Nehemiah made two strategic requests of the king. He knew he not only needed the king's blessing, but also his assistance in this tremendous undertaking. He asked the king for a letter to the governors of the surrounding cities so he would be safe in traveling to Jerusalem and to put the other governors on notice that he had their boss's approval for such an undertaking.

As a result, this letter would also appoint Nehemiah governor of this broken-down city in Judah. His second request was a letter to the keeper of the king's forest to give wood to repair the city and to make a home that he would occupy. The king did all that, plus he sent out the cavalry to protect Nehemiah.

Our tools for the mission after surrendering our financial lives to the Creator is knowing that the life of obedience is not a life of taking away our freedom, but one of unequalled and unparalleled freedom. It is freedom from the pain of financially poor decisions, the freedom of now having margin in your finances.

You will have the freedom from the consuming power of money, and you will also have the freedom from debt. 37 The Word of God describes debt as bondage or of being a slave to the lender.

Thousands of people I have counseled, coached, emailed, or spoken to in groups have expressed the truth of this Scripture.

Our first practical tool is to stop spending.

The way we accomplish this is to know exactly where the money is going and how much is coming in. Take a pad of paper, or download a free thirty-day diary from our website and start recording every cent that comes in and goes out.

This exercise may cure some right off the bat. There are many who would rather not spend than have to write down every cent spent. If that is you, you may have already won, as Publisher's Clearinghouse would say.

Second, we need to control spending to reach our goals.

To reach your goals you have got to know what your goals are and then start a spending plan. We will not use the term budget, because nobody likes it.

This will allow you to better utilize other tools to show you in which areas you need to reduce spending and increase income for a season. As my good friend and fellow financial counselor Stuart Easterly says, "This is the season of sacrifice."

Understand that this will not be forever; this is only boot camp. You will be able to tell yourself, "I, with God's help, can make it during this time of sacrifice." After the season is over and you look back at the time it took to achieve your goals, you will see God's hand as He carried you through many tough times.

Remember, you are obeying God by changing your lifestyle, getting out of debt, and increasing margin in your life.

Third, you need handcuffs.

Once you have a spending plan, you need to place restrictions on yourself. Maybe you have to put yourself on a cash-only system or avoid the places where you are tempted. In order for the spending plan to work, you must adhere to it 100 percent, with no exceptions.

DAY 15

Expect Opposition

"BUT WHEN SANBALLAT THE HORONITE AND TOBIAH THE AMMONITE
OFFICIAL HEARD OF MY ARRIVAL, THEY WERE VERY ANGRY ... ."
(NEHEMIAH 2:10A, NLT)

"IF A PERSON GETS HIS ATTITUDE TOWARD MONEY STRAIGHT, IT WILL
HELP STRAIGHTEN OUT ALMOST EVERY OTHER AREA IN HIS LIFE."
– BILLY GRAHAM

"HE WHO HAS A WHY TO LIVE FOR CAN BEAR ALMOST ANY HOW."
– FRIEDRICH NIETZSCHE

Achieving this goal is too important to quit. Nehemiah's first obstacle was facing the king, his boss. And, of course, the queen weighed in too. There is simply a different atmosphere when the discussion is man to man, versus employee to employer and wife. Things that men don't think of are spoken. It is just a fact. When a man gets off the phone with someone, his wife asks, "So, what did he say?" We men say, "Not much." The wife responds, "What do you mean? You were on the phone for fifteen minutes."

We mention about ten seconds of data that we pared down and invariably our spouse says, "Did you ask about ...?

What do we say?

"Well, no, I didn't ask that. We spoke about other important stuff."

The wife invariably says, "Well, what about ...?"

We say, "Actually, we didn't talk about that either."

Then she says, "Well, what *did* you talk about?"

This is usually the gist of the hubby-and-wife differences.

Now, ratchet that up a few notches. After Nehemiah speaks, the king is probably getting the eyebrow look, and then the nod, and perhaps the whisper. This is where Nehemiah had to be completely in God's zone, because the king asked a question that most men would never, ever think about nor answer correctly. "How long will your journey take and when will you get back?"[38] How long will it take for you to tackle the improbable or impossible?

Don't know? How about fifty-two days? If Nehemiah could get the city jump-started in fifty-two days, then, you, with God's help, can get your financial fortress on track so that the enemy does not deliver the final deathblow.

I have to warn you, folks are not going to like what you are doing. Plain and simple, people will be jealous, greedy, opinionated, and the list goes on. We've all been there. We have been on both sides, unfortunately. It is time to expect opposition and expect God's amazing hand to bring us through or to bring us home. Either way, we end up as the winner.

Nehemiah had two constant foes and these unsavory characters were a cross between Hitler and a used-car salesman, all wrapped up in warped and twisted minds. The two characters were Sanballat the Horonite and Tobiah the Ammonite. They heard someone wanted to promote the welfare of the Israelites. They were very disturbed—literally and mentally.[39]

The plot thickens …

Who are your adversaries? Is it the corporate jealousy, the backbiting neighbors, the vicious family members, the uncaring bill collectors, or the spouse that seems to blame you for everything? Rest assured, the evil one will roll out new and relentless obstacles when you take these steps to honor the king. But, as in Nehemiah's case, God protected him and continued to do so even amidst tremendous odds. Remember that your God does not care what the odds are. He makes the odds.

DAY 16

Surveying the Damage

" ... SO I WENT UP THE VALLEY BY NIGHT, EXAMINING THE WALL ... ."
(NEHEMIAH 2:15)

"THE POINT IS, LADIES AND GENTLEMEN, THAT GREED—FOR LACK OF A
BETTER WORD—IS GOOD. GREED IS RIGHT. GREED WORKS."
- GORDON GECKO IN WALL STREET

"THE TASK AHEAD OF YOU IS NEVER AS GREAT AS THE
POWER BEHIND YOU." - AUTHOR UNKNOWN

Nehemiah opened up his ride and with maximum horsepower he rode.[40] He was not escaping the inevitable but going into it and assessing the situation.

What courage. What a real man. What a fool!

A fool?

Yeah, what man would go face to face with the financial wreckage in his life with the absolute resolve that he was going to follow God no matter how long it would take to restore a classic.

We're not talking about an old car.

I have a good friend who has been working on a 1935 Model T. He and his son have put in an air conditioner, reupholstered the seats, installed a new dashboard, put on a zillion coats of paint, and logged hours upon hours rubbing and buffing this old classic.

But Nehemiah was not restoring a classic in his free time as a hobby. This was much bigger. He was at the crossroads of his life. He could either follow the God of the universe and be used by Him to do something extraordinary or go back to his comfort zone.

How about you? Are you ready to go on an adventure that will show the world your God is good, not gold?

DAY 17

There Will Be Blood ...
or at Least Jealousy

"... THEY WERE VERY MUCH DISTURBED THAT SOMEONE HAD COME TO
PROMOTE THE WELFARE OF THE ISRAELITES ... ." (NEHEMIAH 2:10)

"OF ALL BAD MEN RELIGIOUS BAD MEN ARE THE WORST." – C.S. LEWIS

"WHEN WILL THE RICH AND THE LEARNED AND THE WISE RENOUNCE
THEIR SHALLOW FRIVOLITY AND GO TO LIVE AMONG THE POOR, THE
IGNORANT, THE OUTCAST AND THE LOST, AND WRITE THEIR ETERNAL
FAME ON THE SOULS BY THEM BLESSED AND BROUGHT TO THE SAVIOR;
THOSE WHO HAVE TASTED THIS HIGHEST JOY—THE JOY OF THE LORD—
WILL NEVER AGAIN ASK IS LIFE WORTH LIVING."
– JOHN PATON, MISSIONARY

"MONEY IS IN SOME RESPECTS LIFE'S FIRE: IT IS A VERY EXCELLENT
SERVANT, BUT A TERRIBLE MASTER." – P.T. BARNUM

Someone out there is not rooting for you. There are those who are hoping you are not serious and that you will give up. Some may be plotting to harm you, sabotage your plan to fast track your debt reduction, your goals of simple living, saving like the ant, and investing in long-lasting pleasure which will in fact help others. Why wouldn't someone support this vision? Perhaps it is jealously, anger, revenge, or maybe it is just hard to comprehend.

Nehemiah was embarking on the selfless, Mother Theresa route. Who in their right mind would oppose that? Sanballat and Tobiah, that's who! Two clowns: one a governor and the other an official of a neighboring town. They were "very much disturbed" that someone would try to help these people. [41]

Politically, their fiefdom was threatened with a new sheriff in town looking to restore a burned-down neighborhood. Strangely, these guys were of the same background, so the opposition was not religious. Just forty years earlier, in 586 BC, Nehemiah's people were treated as mere property and the girls and boys traded for fleeting pleasures. [42]

It is easy to say we are being persecuted for our faith, but in most of North, Central, and South America this just is not true. We have the freedom to worship God freely, but many do not. It is estimated that almost half of the world's population, approximately three billion people, face persecution if they attend a service to study God's Word and to worship Jesus Christ. [43]

But this wasn't the case for Nehemiah. It was old-fashioned jealously and fear of someone new moving in on Sanballat and Tobiah's territory.

Your financial life may not seem quite as significant as Nehemiah's great adventure, but God is just as interested in you and the life He has given you as He was in the lives of His prophets of old. Your opposition may be people at work or family who may be jealous or predatory creditors taking advantage of you or just that person in your life who says you'll never amount to much. Here is what God says, "Open wide your mouth and I will fill it ..." (Psalm 81:10b). Solomon in Ecclesiastes 2:26, gives this promise: "To the man who pleases Him, God gives wisdom, knowledge, and happiness."

You will receive opposition in following God, but He promises a joy and a peace that is only found in handling money His way.

DAY 18

Are You With Me?

"THEN I SAID TO THEM, 'YOU SEE THE TROUBLE WE ARE IN: JERUSALEM
LIES IN RUINS, AND ITS GATES HAVE BEEN BURNED WITH FIRE. COME, LET
US REBUILD THE WALL OF JERUSALEM, AND WE WILL NO LONGER BE IN
DISGRACE.' I ALSO TOLD THEM ABOUT THE GRACIOUS HAND OF MY GOD
UPON ME AND WHAT THE KING HAS SAID TO ME. THEY REPLIED,
'LET US START REBUILDING' ..." (NEHEMIAH 2:17-18).

"WHILE MONEY CAN'T BUY HAPPINESS, IT CERTAINLY LETS YOU CHOOSE
YOUR OWN FORM OF MISERY." – GROUCHO MARX

"OH, THAT THE PLEASURE-SEEKING MEN AND WOMEN OF THE WORLD
WOULD ONLY TASTE AND FEEL THE REAL JOY OF THOSE WHO KNOW
AND LOVE THE TRUE GOD, A HERITAGE WHICH THE WORLD CANNOT GIVE
TO THEM BUT WHICH THE POOREST AND HUMBLEST OF FOLLOWERS OF
JESUS KNOW." – JOHN PATON, MISSIONARY

I am reminded of a classic line from C.S. Lewis's *The Chronicles of Narnia: The Lion, the Witch, and the Wardrobe*. Just before the great battle between good and evil, the boy-king Peter says to the half-horse, half-man creature who pledged to fight alongside the sons of Adam, "Are you with me?" A simple "Yes, sir" or "I think" or "Why not?" would have sufficed, but this involved life and death.

He turned to Peter and said, "Until the death." That is devotion. Someone who says, "I believe in you, I am with you, and I will fight for you until the finish line or till death, whichever comes first" is devoted to you.

Nehemiah went back to the people and said two things. Strategically, the first was the glaringly obvious: "We are in desperate trouble. This place is a mess and has literally been burnt down. Let's rebuild it to get out of this awful disgrace."[44]

Second, Nehemiah said God had been very good to him and opened up many doors that could not have been opened by human hands. Even the king himself had written letters to help. God had done some incredible miracles and even used a man who had no incentive to come to their aid.

Now write down ten essential financial miracles that you need and make a promise to God that you will not presume upon Him or rescue Him. If He forgets His checkbook, you do not have to swipe your credit card. He owns the cattle on a thousand hills. He also owns the silver and gold, so if your god forgets his checkbook you better upgrade to a bigger God today. [45]

Next time you are at that familiar crossroad, the one where you have the choice to charge something you "need," your mind says, "I have a brain and a credit card so I will swipe it." God has not designed us for this type of spiritual conflict. Trusting God does not mean going without our needs. God has promised to take care of our needs and give us joy, peace, and hope through *all* of the hills and valleys we traverse.

Our minds say, "This can't be true." Our hearts have always said, "I wish it were true." It is true. Trust Him this time!

DAY 19

"Now Who's First?"

"ELIASHIB THE HIGH PRIEST AND HIS FELLOW PRIESTS WENT TO WORK AND REBUILT THE SHEEP GATE. THEY DEDICATED IT AND SET ITS DOORS IN PLACE ... ." (NEHEMIAH 3:1)

"I'M LIVING SO FAR BEYOND MY INCOME THAT WE MAY ALMOST BE SAID TO BE LIVING APART." – E.E. CUMMINGS

Don't get me wrong. There are many leaders, pastors, bosses, coaches, and cheerleaders who are willing to get their proverbial hands dirty, but the old *lead by example* has its limits.

"You don't expect me to begin swabbing the deck first, do you?"

"I don't mind helping out but, as you know, I have paid my dues. Now someone else needs to experience the toilet-cleaning ministry."

The problem is that the way the world and the media see pastors is, at best, not much different from them, and, at worst, greedy for gain, covetous of power, and lustful for pleasure.

You may not be concerned about looking different from the rest of the world but, if you are like most people, you have a deep desire to live a life that is significant, a life that is original. [46]

In Nehemiah's day they didn't get together to discuss who was in charge, who was the most important among them, who was dunked, sprinkled, or splashed, or who was the most impressive. They simply heard the God-given vision from an obedient servant who was absolutely unqualified to rebuild a city, let alone be a governor. Nehemiah was a mansion- dwelling, Chardonnay-server, not a Gatorade-gulping construction worker.

This all changed, though. This was no New Year's resolution to remodel the kitchen; this was the time to say, "I will no longer live for comfort as I inch closer and closer to death. I will do what I was created to do."

In Nehemiah's day, the first to begin the work were the pastors. They led by example. How do you motivate volunteers who have limited time, resources, and vision? You start with a vision that is from God, and this small point cannot be overlooked. Then prepare your house, family, and finances around this adventure for a massive life change. Then convey the vision and be the first to volunteer. If your people do not follow, either you will be a Noah and only you and your family will finish, or perhaps the vision is not God's vision.

People on this planet are yearning for more than a vision; they wake up every day looking for what may satisfy a deep longing that is being anesthetized by comfort. A longing poorly paved over every day by things that please temporarily: the clothes, the furniture, the cars, the electronics, the food, the holiday, the fling, and the laughs. But what if the yearning could be scratched and satisfied? Add one more layer to it.

What if you held the secret? Would you get high on your own supply? Absolutely. That is what Nehemiah, his pastors, and his people did and the whole world watched in wonder. Some watched in anger and horror.

You know what time it is. Tomorrow when you wake up, decide to live your life intentionally and with singular passion. Live a life that is completely focused on managing money God's way.

Two events have been tattooed in my memory and all involve pastors who swam upstream from the current of cynicism. The first was the pastor of an International Bible Baptist Church where I was speaking one Saturday. During the event there was an older-looking gentleman taking out garbage, setting up chairs, and cleaning up spills in the back of the large auditorium. He looked like the cleaning guy; he was sporting jeans and an old tee shirt. I greeted him a few times because it seems like the workers are usually my best friends wherever I go.

Finally, I ran into him again and he introduced himself as the pastor of this church of over 1,000 members.

I said, "You are the head cheese, the top dog? What are you doing cleaning up the garbage?"

He said, "I am just pitching in, doing what needs to be done to make this day the best it can be."

I was blown away. The senior pastor was getting his hands dirty without regard for what it looked like to a passerby.

The second event that will be forever etched in my heart involved a Pentecostal Church of God in Christ pastor, Bishop Randy Hightower of West Palm Beach, Florida. It was another event where I was speaking that included a meal—food and caffeine are the usual fare when I speak; it helps keep people awake.

I noticed the pastor slipping out a bit early, but thought nothing of it. He probably had important things to do.

He did.

During a break I went to a solitary place looking for the green room and stumbled upon the kitchen. I peeked through the door and saw a man bent over several commercial sized pots on a hot stove, sweating like an iron chef. Not racing against the clock, but competing against discomfort while laboring in love. I saw potatoes being chopped, water boiling, and meat cooking—all without the help of a sous-chef. I wondered if this guy was a volunteer or a hired gun brought in to serve a hundred-plus meals.

I couldn't just stare, so I said hello.

He turned and said, "You are doing a great job and I have been praying for you; this is exactly what my people need."

I said, "Pastor, is that you?"

Behind the steam and the sweat I saw a senior pastor who knew how to capture the hearts of his people and lead by great example.

Maybe you're next. What if, like Nehemiah, God has a life-changing plan for your company, your church, your family, or your life?

Solomon jotted this truth about His God, "Commit to the Lord whatever you do, and your plans will succeed."[47]

Start now on a plan to live below your means, conquer and avoid debt, save regularly and give radically. A spending plan is the way to accomplish these lifelong fundamentals. If your plan is to indulge yourself with things that will end up being painful, don't expect Solomon's words to be your trump card to cajole God. In the words of Jesus' brother James, "When you ask, you do not receive, because you ask with wrong motives, that you may spend what you get on your pleasures."[48]

Live in obedience and honor the King, and He will make getting out of debt, living below your means, saving, and investing in the kingdom pleasureful.

DAY 20

Seriously, How Did They Do It in 52 Days?

"Above the Horse Gate, the priests made repairs, each in front of his own house. Next to them, Zadok son of Immer made repairs opposite his house. Next to him, Shemaiah ... made repairs. Next to him, Hananiah ... repaired another section. Next to them, Meshullam ... made repairs opposite his living quarters ... ." (Nehemiah 3:28-30)

"Every great work, every great accomplishment, has been brought into manifestation through holding to the vision, and often just before the big achievement comes apparent failure and discouragement." – Florence Scovel Shinn

"The rich are the scum of the earth in every country." – G.K. Chesterton

You must be kidding. You mean to tell me that Nehemiah got everyone repairing, rebuilding, and remodeling his or her own part of the wall? Ingenious! Nehemiah pulled a Tom Sawyer, but he didn't sit back and fish.

Nehemiah and his people started this journey of a thousand steps with the undeniable call from God to accomplish a great task with people who had a great stake in the success of the project.

This was a critical element in the fortress being rebuilt. It is a critical element in your financial fortress being completed, too.

They worked on the walls behind their own homes. They didn't mind who owned what and where their property ended and someone else's property began; they worked on their part of the wall and helped their neighbors work on their part of the wall.

This financial fortress will require the entire family behind the mission. This is not the time to allow pride to sabotage the mission.

It is time to come clean with the family. Bring them into the equation. There is nothing like having your loved ones with you to lend a hand and bring some reality and maybe even some levity to the situation.

You say you can't tell the entire family where you have been and where you must go? You think they are too young, too fragile, too condemning, too condescending?

Roger thought so too. He knew he was worth more dead than alive.

Roger was a missionary with a secret. He had been using credit cards a lot and was embarrassed to reveal this to his wife. The excuse he gave was her fragile health. Emotionally she may not be able to handle the shock and the pressure of facing the consequences of their already-stretched household finances.

Roger sank deeper and deeper into debt. He would get to the mailbox before his wife and hide the bills before she could see them. His nerves were getting frayed and he hated living this life of deceit.[49] Not enough to come clean, though.

His only other option was to continue to be deceived as he deceived.

The mission had petty cash that he was in charge of administering—money that was supposed to be used to purchase items necessary for the mission when checks were either not available or not accepted. There was always an ample supply. He would never have borrowed a cent if he didn't have a plan to repay within a day. The day grew to two days, then a week, then a month, and on and on.

Now he was even more afraid to come clean with his wife and family. He was a missionary, a man of God. He could hear the sneers and jeers of those who wait for such a moment when one of God's children falls. Then they can scoff at them and announce to the world how followers of Christ are all hypocrites and insincere and greedy for gain.

He was unable to work or function or even live. His last-ditch effort was to deliver himself into the hands of a sovereign God who has the power to snuff out life and or to deliver those facing a certain death.

What would He do in this situation? What would you do? Is it true that "a bruised reed he will not break"?[50] Roger was not prepared to face this question mark in his soul.

He examined the life insurance papers. There was no suicide clause. He was free to explore all options. The amount of the life insurance proceeds far exceeded the amount he now owed. His wife and boys would have a clean start. This would be one last attempt at a solution. He had heard that Larry Burkett's organization, Crown Financial Ministries, had financial counselors. He received my name and we met at my office one day.

"I am worth more dead than alive," he exclaimed with tears welling up in his eyes. I was speechless, and I love to talk. He said his wife was not able to hear about the debts and then he showed me the financial damage. It brought the whole situation to a sobering climax for a critical decision. God's megaphone was blaring.

I did not know what to say, so I suggested we pray. I don't remember what I prayed but I do remember the pull of my heart to draw God closer to both of us. I was begging for His wisdom.

All I could say, as he showed me his financial mess, was that God would allow his wife to receive this information without the devastating results that appeared to be far worse than suicide. We then prayed specifically for his wife and family.

Waiting to hear the verdict was like waiting for a death-row pardon call from the governor.

He called and said, "You will not believe this! My wife said she was with me and that God would get us through and that we could even sell the townhouse to pay off the debts because I was more important to her than the house."

Roger's faith was stretched that day and so was mine. He is now debt free, completely transparent, and effecting massive life-change in more lives than he will ever know.

Have a family meeting to bring everyone up to speed. I know, you live in the real world, not a *Leave It to Beaver* world. That is fine, but the family meeting may take on a fairly different dynamic than what you may expect.

Author Nick Morgan, who wrote *Working the Room*,[51] says to start with communicating the problem and then take your family from *why* there must be change to *how* this change can be accomplished.

Rest assured, God will give you the strength to go toe to toe against the status quo. Everyone needs to know you mean business and it is not about your agenda this time; it is about His.

DAY 21

Storming the Gates

Ten critical gateways into the city were all feverishly rebuilt in record time. They were all repaired by residents, not professionals. They were racing, not against each other to build bigger barns; they were racing against the clock, against an attack that could not only destroy their city, but their lives! [52]

A few doors repaired? That doesn't seem very noteworthy. These were not just repainted closet doors; these were pressure points that could ultimately cause the city to sink or rise. Nehemiah did not have to tell his people where they were most vulnerable, they knew it inherently; they had been down this road before. This time there would be no leaks, no holes, no compromises, no mistakes. The lives of many depended on each person.

Years later, men from Greece, the Athenians, could relate to this type of threat. They were under siege by the wicked and world-conquering Persians. Outnumbered ten to one, the Athenians sent their fastest messenger, Phidippides, 150 miles to Sparta to ask the Spartans to join them in the fight of their lives. The Spartans said they would not help until the full moon.

When the Persians arrived on the shores of Marathon, villagers, peasants, mothers and fathers, boys and girls all met them and fought for their lives. The Persians fought for something less important. Many were slaves of the Persian Empire and were forced to fight for more land. The Athenians, although ridiculously outnumbered, pushed the Persians back into retreat. In great joy the Athenians sent their fastest man once again to announce the stunning victory. Phidippides ran twenty-six miles from the plains of Marathon to downtown Athens. Upon his arrival and his announcement that Persia was defeated, he dropped dead of exhaustion. The Athenians were nearly invincible because they were fighting for their lives.

You know all too well where your gates are—where you are most tempted financially, where you have the biggest willpower struggle, where you have the scars to prove your financial mistakes. This time will be different. This time you are fighting for your lives. Each time you have made the financial decision to follow the path of the advertisers, the Joneses, or the deep knowledge that satisfaction is but a purchase away, you have come one step closer to a certain financial death.

Your gates are being stormed even as you read this. It is time to shore up the gates, to repair the most embattled areas of your financial life. Which is it? Too much house? Eating out? A car? Gambling? Electronics? Clothes? Your kids?

Make a list of your vulnerable areas and pray daily that you would avoid the temptation to indulge in these places. Don't drive by Starbucks if you have a problem with spending too much there. Don't pass your favorite store at the mall. Duck, jive, and dodge giving in to temptation in those susceptible areas in your life.

In America, we spend approximately an obscene $600 billion on automobiles each year, $40.8 billion on pet paraphernalia, $20 billion on ice cream, $110 billion on fast food, and $33 billion on diets.53 Meanwhile, almost half of the world's more than six billion people live on less than two dollars a day. More than 600 million will die of starvation and even worse, of those who will die, 70 percent do not know Jesus Christ.

Creamy coffee, a comfy Civic, or an investment that will pay off forever: which will it be? I love coffee, but I will curb my caffeine intake for a new Civic. Really, though, what is wrong with my old Civic? Perhaps I can buy used and invest the difference in life change.

Ask yourself what pays more eternal dividends in the long run.

DAY 22

What Do Gold and Perfume Have in Common?

"Uzziel son of Harhaiah, one of the goldsmiths, repaired the next section; and Hananiah, one of the perfume-makers, made repairs next to that. They restored Jerusalem as far as the Broad Wall." (Nehemiah 3:8)

"Teamwork is the ability to work together toward a common vision. The ability to direct individual accomplishments toward organizational objectives. It is the fuel that allows common people to attain uncommon results." – Andrew Carnegie

"Someday I want to be rich. Some people get so rich they lose all respect for humanity. That's how rich I want to be." – Rita Rudner

Uzziel and Hananiah are both critical to the wall being built. No, the fortress was not built in gold and did not smell like Old Spice. Gold and perfume represented the day jobs for a couple of families that now were calling this city-under-construction their home. Nehemiah had two unlikely construction teams on the clock: the folks with the family-run jewelry shop and the rather nice-smelling family who owned and operated the local Perfumania franchise in the mall.

Imagine the looks on the faces of the jeweler and the perfume maker when they were given their assignments to work outside on the house and fence. I am sure they thought to themselves more than once, "I'm not sure if my talents are being utilized to their utmost potential in this ministry." At this point some may have gone to Nehemiah and asked whether there was an administrative position that needed to be filled or an executive slot to move into. But here were two neighbors in very different professions, accepting the fifty-two-day challenge to work on their part, so that their neighbors would also be safe.

Bob Coy, the senior pastor at Calvary Chapel in Fort Lauderdale, often speaks of the "cigarette butt ministry." When folks start out volunteering and sharing their gifts and talents with others, some find themselves doing insignificant jobs in the world's eyes, but not in God's eyes. Every job working for the Lord is of equal importance.

You may feel this whole downscaling deal is not what you were born to do. You might feel as if it is not your fault and you are absolutely not willing to live any differently to rebuild your wall. Or perhaps you have done everything you are going to do and God must do the rest. He hasn't asked you to make any more sacrifices. God knows that you enjoy and need your comforts. You can relate with the entrepreneur, jeweler, and perfumer; handyman stuff is way beneath you.

Nehemiah's business people could have felt the same way, but if they had they would be dead. The enemy would have slipped over, or through their stubborn insubordination and probably would have killed both families. When faced with this lopsided prospect, real men and women step up to the plate and experience life-changing miracles. Their courage also causes a ripple effect that often interrupts our lives to let us know that this financial boot camp will not last forever. It is for a short period of time.

By trusting God in this adventure you will not only be securing your financial fortress, but God promises this transaction will bring a return of pleasure, joy, and satisfaction. In a world of temporary peace and momentary pleasure, it is an absolute necessity to know that because of God's love He wants to deliver the long-term, true contentment-producing, soul-satisfying hope, peace, and incredible joy.

God has completely prepared you for such a task even if it seems you are a square peg in a round hole. Don't think of yourself as a jeweler or a perfume retailer, but as someone uniquely qualified for such a time as this.

John was happily employed by a major food maker. His territory was growing, and his fifteen-plus years made climbing the corporate ladder comfortable, until one day when a friend laid out a plan to start a business. They would be their own bosses. They would have all the good without any of the headaches. He shocked everyone at the company by tendering his resignation.

The new business rented space, purchased equipment, and canvassed for customers. John ran the warehouse and the operations. However, competition was fierce and ruthless and after one year they decided to cut their losses and close the doors of the business.

John had always considered law enforcement and decided to pursue it. He excelled in the police academy and secured a coveted position with a local government agency. After one year as a cop, John found himself out of a job again.

So he did what a man's got to do. He was willing to flip the proverbial burgers and in fact he did. He managed a hamburger joint. He opened, he closed, he cooked, he cleaned, he ate greasy burgers, he delivered for parties, but he was still broke; barely making enough to cover the household bills. He was miserable. Life as he knew it ceased to exist. His family worried about him and he worried about himself. God never left him though. He had a plan. Just like He has a plan for you and the jeweler and the perfume family.

Tired, dejected, at the bottom, and still flipping hamburgers, John constantly looked for a new position that did not involve the smell of greasy meat and burnt fries. But with every interview came more rejection. Then he was called back for a position completely over his head; one that would mean national sales and management responsibility. He was sure this was a big waste of time. He and one hundred really qualified candidates were flown to Atlanta for face-to-face interviews at the corporate office. He did not own a jacket or a suitcase. He was laughing all the way to the airport in his borrowed blazer and bag.

John sat in the waiting room talking to God and saying to himself that he should at least be back home earning something flipping burgers at the greasy spoon. As they called his name, he quickly looked at his watch and thought he might just be able to make a flight and be at work tomorrow morning.

His cheap blazer cut into his neck and caused him to gasp occasionally for air as he was barraged with questions. All he could think of was the poor blokes that had to wear one of these get-ups every day. The interviewers asked him to sit back in the lobby. John borrowed a phone and on the company's dime tried to book a flight back as one by one the other candidates turned and left the corporate offices. Sitting in the lobby, he anticipated the executive's words, "I am sorry, John, although your qualifications were outstanding, we have decided to go with someone else. We will keep your resume in our files, though."

Finally, a well-dressed executive popped her head out of the door and asked him to follow her. Winding down the narrow hallways past cubicle after cubicle, he felt indignant that they wouldn't just shoot straight with him and tell him he was not in the running.

He was asked to sit down with the president of the company who said, "Of course, you're probably wondering why everyone was asked to leave." John really didn't care. He was trying to get a flight back home.

"No, not really, sir." John stated.

"Well, John," said the president, "if your background is correct, we have found our next director of sales."

"You're kidding."

"No, John, your background in large-company merchandizing for fifteen years, your entrepreneurial experience with small businesses, and your security background are all vital. Plus your recent experience in serving the customer day in and day out is exactly what we have been looking for. Now how much do we need to offer you to make it happen?"

John laughed until he cried. God had not abandoned him; He was perfecting him.

The gold and the perfume families surrendered to the perfect plan that God had for them. [53] Your time is now. Buckle up and hunker down. There are rough waters ahead, but downsizing is not to hurt you, but to perfect you.

DAY 23

There Is a Limit to How Much I Can Accomplish!

"THE VALLEY GATE WAS REPAIRED BY HANUN AND THE RESIDENTS OF
ZANOAH. THEY REBUILT IT AND PUT ITS DOORS AND BOLTS AND BARS IN
PLACE. THEY ALSO REPAIRED FIVE HUNDRED YARDS OF THE WALL AS FAR
AS THE DUNG GATE." (NEHEMIAH 3:13)

"KNOW YOUR LIMITS, BUT NEVER ACCEPT THEM." – AUTHOR UNKNOWN

"WHEN I HAVE MONEY, I GET RID OF IT QUICKLY, LEST IT FIND A WAY
INTO MY HEART." – JOHN WESLEY

Hanun and his neighbors repaired almost one-third of a mile of wall. No matter how little the repairs were, that was a task of incredible proportion for folks who were not carpenters, bricklayers, or even handymen. They were ordinary people who did an extraordinary task.

Does this sound vaguely familiar? Does your situation look like a mile-long mess of financial ruin and carnage? Do you think it is impossible without winning the lottery? I am sure these neighbors may have said the same thing if they were not completely convinced that God was going to give them this amazing victory. Nehemiah shared a vision and his people believed it would change their lives. He led by example, and they accomplished awe-inspiring results.

There may be a limit to your strength, but not God's. He will accomplish His goal, whether it is with an individual or a family working beside each other.

We have all heard, "I can do everything through Him who gives me strength." Yeah, but that was then. How can I trust Him for the gray area or the little stuff, like eating, working, staying out of debt, or even getting paid. Real faith is tested in small areas like this.

By taking God's steps you will be honoring Him, and as Solomon penned, "But whoever listen to me will live in safety and be at ease, without fear of harm." The fear you are facing will only get worse if you do nothing. By trusting Him and taking the steps to downsize, decrease spending, increase income (at least temporarily), and look for satisfaction in items you cannot purchase or consume. This whole change of mind toward money is critically important not only to your financial survival, but to all those who watch as well.

Berni was a single mom who struggled for years. She had three small children and an ex-husband who lived out of the country. She received no child support. She would come in for financial coaching month after month and show me a new credit card bill that she had incurred for either food or school clothes for the kids or repairs on her clunker of a car.

I would encourage her to trust God and would quote Solomon's words, "Trust in the Lord with all your heart and lean not on your own understanding."[54] But what do you say, honestly, to a woman who struggles each month to earn enough to rent a cramped apartment in a seedy area, buy groceries, get clothes for her children, and have pizza once in a while? I couldn't blame her for filling out new credit card applications each time she felt the pain of a dissatisfied life, and a need for the necessities and the things the rest of us seem to spend a lifetime pursuing. It is dichotomous; you trust God for the things you cannot buy, as we who can afford these things, indulge.

When will we finally admit that God plus nothing is worthless to us on this planet, but God plus comfort brings a smile to our faces and displaces our fears?

Are you uncomfortable? You should be. I am too. The greatest tragedy a client of mine could face is being broke. What if most of us on this planet have something far worse—a poverty of the soul?

Berni trusted God through years of being single, and had great love from her heavenly Father. Her dad had divorced her mother years ago and she did not have the relationship with him that the Creator had intended. However, a sweet relationship had been built later in life, when she needed it the most.

This time it was with her Father above. She walked daily with Him and her children saw it. They experienced miracles at Christmas in the form of anonymous envelopes with cash. The children are now adults and they remember their mom's faith and the loyalty of their God. God promises to never leave us nor forsake us.[55]

Raised by a mom who was abandoned by the man she trusted the most, they had been unwillingly tutored about being forsaken, a marital word that speaks of infidelity or abandonment. But this Man, the God Man, will never leave you. This gets real when you have nothing left to substitute for Him. Berni was at the point where she had no one to turn to except the greatest treasure and comfort we could ever dream of: Jesus Christ. This time she wasn't let down. She experienced a sacred romance that perhaps only few through history have tasted.

Berni got it. Her contagious faith was rubbing off on others. She is now married and has a passion for helping single moms find their way to a sacred romance with Christ. She leads single moms to trust Him for their daily needs instead of leaning on a new credit card or worse.

Perhaps you are there right now. God has a huge plan for you through this impossible task. It will empower your faith and ignite your passion to be a witness to what God can do with someone who fully follows and values the greatest treasure.

DAY 24

The Little Church That Could

"The men of Jericho built the adjoining section, and Zaccur son of Imri built next to them. The Fish Gate was rebuilt by the sons of Hassenaah. They laid its beams and put its doors and bolts and bars in place. Meremoth ... repaired the next section. Next to him Meshullam ... made repairs, and next to him Zadok ... made repairs" (Nehemiah 3:2-4).

"We are on a mission from God." – Blues Brothers.

"Money is like manure. You have to spread it around or it smells." – J. Paul Getty

Kevin Fisher, the pastor of Berni's church, the Miami Vineyard Community Church, shared a vision one fateful Sunday about collecting an offering for a little inner-city church that was struggling financially. Amazingly, God began to work in the hearts of a great number of people in that humble church.

The temptation to be smart, to use the brain God has given you, and not go overboard did enter their minds. But they remembered where they had been and how faithful and generous God had been.

So they and three hundred others decided to go without, to downsize, to forego an addition, a repair, a blouse, a holiday, and things that satisfy for only a moment. It was risky. It was crazy.

The day arrived. The proverbial offering plates passed from hand to hand around the congregation. Every check, dollar, and coin would be converted to one check made payable to the Centro Christiano Casablanca.

Wednesday was the day to deliver the sacrificial offering. Three hundred adrenalin-filled adventurers crowded in cars, vans, and buses to surprise eight people huddled around a dry marker board with three words scribbled on it: "God will provide." This humble gathering had no idea that 300 crazed congregants would converge on them at any moment.

The doors opened and one by one each person rushed in. They all found seats, their collective body filling the modest church to the rafters. The applause, whistling, talking, and laughing reached a deafening pitch. As if on cue, a hush came over the audience as the stunned pastor of the inner city church, Eddie Rivera, made his way to the stage and said just ten words, "Pastor, I just want to know what is going on!" Pastor Kevin from the Vineyard took the microphone from Pastor Eddie's hand and spoke a deep spiritual truth to the anxious crowd, "In the words of the great theologians, the Blues Brothers, we are on a mission from God!" The excitement could no longer be contained. The house of worship erupted in an awe-inspiring cacophony of screams, cheers, and shouts.

Pastor Kevin reached into his pocket and pulled out the envelope that contained the offering. Pastor Eddie's next words could barely be heard above the din of the crowd as he opened the envelope and read its contents: "It is more blessed to give than receive. Here is your check for fifty-seven-thousand dollars." These last words came out fitfully as he fought back the tears his wife had already given into.

Exuberant tears began to flow down the faces of too many to count. No one knew this, but Pastor Eddie had not been paid for six months. An air-conditioning repairman who was not a Christian happened to be at the church fixing the forever-broken air-conditioning unit. He was so moved by this selfless act, he gave his life to the Lord that very day.

These initial repercussions were only beginning. Hundreds of thousands have seen the homemade video taken at Centro Christiano and have given their lives to Christ, and many other churches have decided to follow Miami Vineyard's example.[56]

Isaiah wrote that God's Word does not "... return to me empty."[57] I once thought that meant it will accomplish something, even if it is small. I now have a new perspective on this truth. The point is, your actions may seem insignificant and petty at the time, but God can use them in exponential ways. Remember this as you are faithful with God's money in paying back your debts or using what God has given you for a higher purpose

DAY 25

There Are Always Those Who Will Not Get Their Hands Dirty

"THE NEXT SECTION [OF THE FORTRESS] WAS REPAIRED BY THE MEN OF TEKOA, BUT THEIR NOBLES WOULD NOT PUT THEIR SHOULDERS TO THE WORK ... ." (NEHEMIAH 3:5)

"DO MORE THAN BELONG: PARTICIPATE. DO MORE THAN CARE: HELP. DO MORE THAN BELIEVE: PRACTICE. DO MORE THAN BE FAIR: BE KIND. DO MORE THAN FORGIVE: FORGET. DO MORE THAN DREAM: WORK."
– WILLIAM ARTHUR WARD

"WHEN IT IS A QUESTION OF MONEY, EVERYBODY IS OF THE SAME RELIGION." – VOLTAIRE

Perhaps most "sheeple" will go the way of the important people of Tekoa ... or Toledo, Tulsa, Tampa, Toronto, Traverse City, Tokyo or your town by some other letter than T. It is so much easier to ignore the situation or hope someone else will do the leg work so we can get on with life. But the "Clean up on Aisle 3" is not punishment nor is it beneath us; it is the way to the top. Just like in Nehemiah's day, the stakes are high. But those who thought more of themselves than others were actually shooting themselves in the foot. They thought this was a job for the little people, but this was a high calling, a holy moment that would define, unite, and inspire an entire generation.

Unfortunately for them they would miss out on a mission with eternal consequences. The truth for us to ponder is one posed by Dr. Charles Stanley, a truth that sums up what we are made of: "Obey God and leave the consequences to Him."[58]

Who are we? Are we what we have become in this life, in our jobs, and in what car we drive? Do we measure our self-worth by our net worth? If there is any deviation in our lifestyle, would it appear to others in our sphere of influence as if we had lost it and fallen off the deep end?

Perhaps we are impressing the wrong people, and need to see ourselves the way the Father sees us—with complete, unchanging, unconditional love and acceptance, with a plan for us that is individually tailored. This is so we may become more Christ-like, not that we would become our own god. That is not what I am saying. The nobles were their own gods and were not Christ-like.

In Romans 8:29, God calls us to bear a resemblance to Christ, not to surpass Him or compete with Him but to illuminate and magnify Him. It's like looking at a comet through a high-powered telescope—like reducing something so big down to a size that our limited brains and eyes can get around in order to appreciate the splendor and majesty and awesomeness.

How does this happen in our financial world? You might have met just that person. He or she is blissfully ignorant of the impending financial doom, or worse; they are chasing the next sale, the next commission. I recently met a man who said he loves the hunt, closing the deal, the big sale. That is what brings him happiness. Like striving for that next injection of pleasure that wears off like a shot of Novocain for a root canal, only this is much more habit-forming. The problem is you must re-anesthetize that area of your heart to keep the pleasure heightened.

What if the nobles could experience an even greater pleasure while also joining in a movement that would more than inspire, it would transform lives forever. God wants to do something similar in your life, in your relationships, and in your finances.

You will never know what God has in store for you if you walk away. You will always be haunted by the question, "What would have happened if I had followed Christ and trusted in His plan?"

Live original. Live lives that are set apart in your financial life![59]

DAY 26

Girl Power

"SHALLUM SON OF HALLOHESH, RULER OF A HALF-DISTRICT OF
JERUSALEM, REPAIRED THE NEXT SECTION WITH THE HELP OF HIS
DAUGHTERS." (NEHEMIAH 3:12)

"WE OUGHT TO CHANGE THE LEGEND ON OUR MONEY FROM 'IN GOD
WE TRUST' TO 'IN MONEY WE TRUST.' BECAUSE, AS A NATION, WE'VE
GOT FAR MORE FAITH IN MONEY THESE DAYS THAN WE DO IN GOD."
– ARTHUR HOPPE

"A WOMAN IS LIKE A TEA BAG, YOU CAN'T TELL HOW STRONG SHE IS
UNTIL YOU PUT HER IN HOT WATER." – NANCY REAGAN

Rent-a-Husband, Inc. is a company that caters to, believe it
or not, busy women who do not have the time or the desire
to tackle leaks, repairs, doors that don't shut, or a deck
that needs painting. These are Rent-a-Husband's quintessential
customers that transformed a once-homeless guy into the owner
of a thirteen-million-dollar-a-year business.[60]
This city and this wall, though, had no handymen or
subcontractors to call. They had something much better. They
had girl power. While nobles were much too important to lift a
finger and get dirty, others caught a glimpse of the big picture.[61]
The daughters of the councilman/mayor could have easily opted
to stay home and watch the workers do the work. These ladies
did no such thing. These gals were the real deal. Not only was
this a unified mission, a singular purpose to accomplishing the
impossible, but a defining moment for all.

Without the passion and sweat-equity of the women, the call would have failed and this part of the city could not have been rebuilt. If it were not for Shallum's daughters, a vulnerable spot would have remained in a most prominent location—the mayor's back yard.

They would have made the news, been on the cover of such ancient publications as "Walls Street Journal," "New Fortress Times Newspaper," "Popular Repairs Magazine," "Ladies Wall Journal," "Sabbath Evening Post," "Home & Cracks Magazine," "Readers Dig & Rest," or "Fortress Illustrated." Why? Because this was not a task completed by human hands, this was a mission that linked ordinary people with an extraordinary God.

Afraid? Beneath you? Uncertain how? Not in for this adventure? The Creator has orchestrated this mission as a call for you. Yes you, ladies. You can be part of a single passion that will be the determining factor in the survival of you and your family's finances.

There is more than meets the eye riding on your passion for seeing God's plan of hope, peace, and joy in how you live with money. It can either own you or you can make it your tool for massive life-change, beginning with your life. This is your first step.

Know your true financial score, not the false god of the credit score. This has duped many people into borrowing for things they don't need, with money they don't have, to impress people that don't care about them, all to increase the great credit score that promises peace and financial security and delivers heartache and headache. This financial score is where you are—the debt, the income, or the assets that you may have to dump to get rid of the pain. Once you have your list, you can know beyond a shadow of a doubt that you can trust God.

Her name is not known but her story is timeless. As matter of fact, her story has been used as an example of faith for over 2,000 years. Jesus knew who to go to for a real example of trust. A woman, who, in the world's eyes, did not have it all together.

Her marriage was broken, she was single, probably had a child or two, and she was broke. The story picks up at church, of all places.[62]

It was that rather uncomfortable moment when the offering plate is passed, the time when music is played to take the edge off the awkward moment until it passes. In this place of worship the offering plates were in the back, like buckets, so when you left you could casually drop something in on the sly if you were so inclined.

That day, though, there were those who were there to be seen and recognized and to have the paparazzi take note of their large bills going into the offering baskets. Unfortunately for the *platinum* contributors, whose dough was there for show, the single mom was there too. It must have been aggravating.

The nerve of this indigent woman ruining their moment! Someone else noticed too, and He had a thing or two say about this inequity. Unfortunately for the showboats it was God with skin: Jesus Christ. He said to His followers, "You see that poor woman?" They must have thought about the poor lady standing there among the *real* givers. "Yeah, that is one sorry-looking sight."

The woman put in two pennies.[63]

All they could do was stare. Then the God-man said something confusing. He said the poor single mom had given more than all the others. More? Surely you jest? You don't mean the poor lady gave more than the wealthy, do you, Jesus? Yeah, that is exactly what He meant. He said these showboats gave out of their wealth, a tip, chump change, coins from the penthouse sofa. The poor widow put in more because she gave all she had. She gave everything. Everything? Yes, everything. What a fool! No one in their right mind, especially a single mom, gives every cent to a church, or a ministry, or a homeless guy, or to spreading the message of Christ to the remotest parts of the globe. Right?

It sounds like she was brainwashed, because no one who is intelligent does something like that. No one except a woman who completely trusts in her man—not just any man, but the Man, who came to Earth to show every woman (and man for that matter) that there is one Man that can be trusted, one Man that will not let them down, one Man that will never leave them or cheat on them.[64]

The poor widow, or the struggling single mom, or any woman who cannot see the end of the financial heartache she is facing can do like the foolish widow because she knew whom she could trust, even with her last cent.

Now be like the mayor's daughters—trust Him for the financial mission of your life that will have a ripple effect throughout eternity. You can do it. God wired you perfectly for the task ahead.

DAY 27

Finishing the Dirtiest of Jobs

"The Dung Gate was repaired by Malkijah son of Racab, ruler of the district of Beth Hakkerem. He rebuilt it and put its doors and bolts and bars in place." (Nehemiah 3:14)

"We shall neither fail nor falter; we shall not weaken or tire... give us the tools and we will finish the job."
– Winston Churchill

"Those who set out to serve both God and mammon soon discover that there is no God." – Logan Pearsall Smith

Of all accomplishments to report upon in the rebuilding of the wall, the Dung Gate may, at first glance, seem the least pleasant. Nonetheless, it is written that, "The Dung Gate was repaired by Malkijah son of Recab, ruler of the district of Beth Hakkerem. He rebuilt it and put its doors and bolts and bars in place."[65] It is strange that such a high-ranking official placed this distasteful piece of the puzzle squarely on his own shoulders.

Did he enjoy it? Did he want to do it? Was he born to do this type of work? Probably not. But he knew the goal was significant enough to warrant any minor bathroom cleaning. He didn't say, "I am too important to be saddled with such menial work as janitorial duty."

What dirty job are you dreading? Are you putting anything off because it is too nasty to tackle right now? It could be a ten-year-old bill or a family member you owe money to or a current debt. Maybe God is leading you to pay back debts that have been discharged. I know this is crazy and if people find out you are paying old debts that you have no legal obligation to pay, they are going to think you have lost your mind and are just plain dumb and legalistic. Remember to separate *legal* and *moral*; "The wicked borrow and do not repay, but the righteous give generously" (Psalm 37:21). Take a page from Malkijah; roll up your sleeves in your mind, toughen up, and handle these problems now.

Or perhaps it is that fear of downsizing. It is that voice in your mind that is saying to you, "If you go backwards you will never, ever, be able to ... buy in this neighborhood, buy a car this nice, send you kids to private school, ..." It is the same voice that says, "You can't do it, give it up, you are a loser." It is from the author of lies, the deceiver, the accuser, the liar—Satan. The voice of truth says, "This is for My glory." The voice of truth says, "Do not be afraid." True and powerful words put to music in the Casting Crowns song "Voice of Truth."

Contact the people you owe money to and tell them you can afford to give them fifty dollars a month, twenty-five dollars a month, ten dollars a month, or maybe only five dollars. Everyone can do this. I don't care what your personal situation is. It doesn't matter. You can do this. Take whatever you have coming in after you have reduced your living expenses to the American basics, and put it toward your debts.

God promises to provide all of your needs, so therefore He will provide it or we don't need it. Imagine saying this and actually believing it. It really is that simple and, as a result, you will see God in a whole different way—as a God who honestly and personally cares for you even in the small areas like money.

So fear not. Downsize to a better life, a richer life, and a life of greater hope.

Do the dirty work and others will see who your God is.

DAY 28

More Opposition

"WHEN SANBALLAT HEARD THAT WE WERE REBUILDING THE WALL,
HE BECAME ANGRY AND WAS GREATLY INCENSED.
HE RIDICULED THE JEWS ... ." (NEHEMIAH 4:1)

"IT IS THE REFORMER WHO IS ANXIOUS FOR THE REFORM, AND NOT
SOCIETY, FROM WHICH HE SHOULD EXPECT NOTHING BETTER THAN
OPPOSITION, ABHORRENCE AND MORTAL PERSECUTION."
– MAHATMA GANDHI

"MONEY DOESN'T TALK, IT SWEARS." – BOB DYLAN

Expect it. When the three stooges—Sanballat, Tobiah, and Geshem—heard that Nehemiah was continuing to rebuild the fortress, they jeered, sneered at, and even used racial slurs against the builders. One of the comments that was made in front of an entire group of people was, "Who do these feeble Jews think they are?" Sanballat even made fun of the way they worshiped God.

He ridiculed the wall, saying, "What, are they going to make sacrifices on top of these walls because they certainly cannot be used as real walls? They will snap their fingers and finish in a day!"

Tobiah chimed in and said that even if a fox climbed up on their wall it would fall down. They laughed until they cried. People of all ages smirked at the wall-builders, telling jokes, shaking heads, and walking away.

They said embarrassing things. They insulted them. They called them names. When they found out they would not stop working, those who opposed Nehemiah got angry. So they plotted to attack Nehemiah and his people.

You know what Nehemiah did first? He went for help, right to the top.[66] Not the king, but the King. Nehemiah poured himself out before God and said something like this: "God, hear us; we are hated and under attack. Would you do to them what they are scheming against us? They are insulting you because you are the builder of this fortress!"

You would think that people would applaud you for wanting to do such a noble task of building margin in your life. But that just is not true. The evil one will not stop, sleep, or rest until you are broke, bankrupt, spent, frustrated, worn-out, and left for dead.

Nehemiah left the fear at the foot of the Cross and trusted his King. When he got up from his heartfelt and laborious prayer, he knew he could go and do the job at hand. And he did.

DAY 29

What Happens When You Work With All of Your Heart?

"SO WE REBUILT THE WALL TILL ALL OF IT REACHED HALF ITS HEIGHT, FOR THE PEOPLE WORKED WITH ALL THEIR HEART."(NEHEMIAH 4:6)

"PLANS ARE ONLY GOOD INTENTIONS UNLESS THEY IMMEDIATELY DEGENERATE INTO HARD WORK." – PETER F. DRUCKER

"MONEY MAY BE THE HUSK OF MANY THINGS BUT NOT THE KERNEL. IT BRINGS YOU FOOD, BUT NOT APPETITE; MEDICINE, BUT NOT HEALTH; ACQUAINTANCE, BUT NOT FRIENDS; SERVANTS, BUT NOT LOYALTY; DAYS OF JOY, BUT NOT PEACE OR HAPPINESS." – HENRIK IBSEN

The prayer was delivered, the plea for help offered, and the request sent to have God avenge His people and to kick their enemies' hind ends for insulting the general contractor who was God himself. The only thing left was to trust God to deliver. Nehemiah knew this so he had a press conference with his ragtag men, women, and children and told them to work like they had never worked before. I am not talking about a forty-hour workweek, with everybody humming and working for the weekend. No, this was life or death.

Nehemiah's people worked with all of their hearts and did what was impossible: they built the wall up to half its height. Sure, it wasn't finished and it was still vulnerable, but the word got out that this little city was serious and they were already halfway there. They didn't start getting cocky; they knew danger was around the corner at every turn. So they focused on the great task at hand because their lives and livelihoods depended on it.

You are at the same crossroad. You can either look at the financial rubble or start rebuilding. What would happen if you decided to work with all of your heart and be completely focused until your wall is rebuilt? You may say, "I would not be able to go to the movies or the mountains or do many of things I want to do." But if you continue to place these important *things* above rebuilding the rubble, people are going to think those things are more important and, more importantly, so will you.

I spoke to a pastor who had some unpaid child support from years ago, before he gave his life to Christ. He asked me if I had any suggestions about paying this enormous amount off more quickly or if he ought to just make the minimum payment which he could do for the rest of his life without paying it completely off. After all, the kids were grown and out of college. It was just a nuisance and a formality to pay the child support division now.

I told him to take a two-year leave of absence from his church, get another job, live on his wife's meager salary, and fully pay this debt. He should modify his lifestyle so much that every available dollar would go toward that debt until it was paid. Then come back to his congregation and see what type of impact it had on them.

He thought I was crazy and I thought that was the end of it. A few months later I got an email from a guy with the same name but whose title read "Sales Rep." He told me he decided to do just what I had suggested and he was excited about what God was going to do for the next few years. Go, God!

Now it is your turn.

DAY 30

Readied for the War?
Pray and Post!

"BUT WHEN [THEY] HEARD THAT THE REPAIRS TO JERUSALEM'S WALLS HAD GONE AHEAD AND THAT THE GAPS WERE BEING CLOSED, THEY WERE VERY ANGRY. THEY ALL PLOTTED TOGETHER TO COME AND FIGHT AGAINST JERUSALEM AND STIR UP TROUBLE AGAINST IT. BUT WE PRAYED TO OUR GOD AND POSTED A GUARD DAY AND NIGHT TO MEET THIS THREAT."(NEHEMIAH 4:7-9)

"THE MORE YOU SWEAT IN PEACETIME, THE LESS YOU BLEED DURING WAR." – CHINESE PROVERB

THAT MONEY TALKS
I'LL NOT DENY,
I HEARD IT ONCE:
IT SAID, "GOODBYE."
– RICHARD ARMOUR

The evil one and his minions are relentless. That is just how it is. However, we have an army of one—one awesome God that will never leave us nor forsake us.[67] Nehemiah was about to experience this phenomenon again.

His people were strong and courageous, right? No! They were sort of like us: scared silly. They said, "Look, Nehemiah, we are weak and tired and we never signed on for this crazy military stuff. We were just fine living where we were. This whole pile of sticks and stones is far too much work. There are piles of crud everywhere. We just can't rebuild this wall. Sorry, nothing against you, pal, but we do not believe in violence. We just want to go home and go to bed."

They also said, in essence, "Not only that but we heard ten times that the bad guys want to sneak up on us and beat us up and maybe even kill us. My wife told me we have got to draw the line someplace and that is now. I still love you, man, but see ya!"

Nehemiah could have buckled. But he didn't. He trusted God. Before everyone could turn and pack and run, he said, "I have a plan." No more running, no more fear, and no more cowardice.[68] We will ready ourselves for battle and we will do it like this. In a courageous moment that has been seen only a handful of times in history, he galvanized the people who were ready to run. He posted entire families with bows and arrows, swords, and spears behind the exposed and most vulnerable places in the wall.

He said, "Don't be afraid of them. Remember the Lord, who is great and awesome, and fight for your brothers, your sons, daughters, wives, and your homes."[69]

What a sight that must have been! Susie with her plastic bow and arrow, little Johnny with his Swiss army knife, and Ma and Pa facing each other, shaking their heads with swords in hand. What if they had to use them?

God to the rescue! When word got out that Nehemiah had gathered his nuclear families together to fight possibly to the death and not back down, the three stooges' (Sanballat, Tobiah, and Gesham) plot was foiled; God had frustrated it.[70] So they backed down and all of Nehemiah's team merrily went back to work on their part of the wall.

This could be your finest moment; this could be the moment that defines you. Will you run or will you stick it out? Nehemiah was immovable and rallied the people with the familiar battle cry, "Don't be afraid of them, God is on your side!"

But you might say, "I wish it were that easy. My enemy is coming after me with subpoenas and summons and lawyers who are worse than snakes. They are not playing fair. It is not as if I am dealing with rational people. You don't know my wife or my husband or my boss or my creditors or the IRS."

Will you trust in the awesome power of God or will you lean on your own understanding? Choose to face this giant and get all the pleasure and give God all the credit.

DAY 31

I Just Can't Do It; I'm Too Tired!

Don't quit now. You are more than halfway there! Sure, times are tough, and you feel like giving up, and there is an enemy out there that is lurking around every corner to tackle you like a linebacker, but this is no game. This is a matter of financial life and death.

I just got a call from Susan and she said she was trying to muster enough courage to call for help. She was at her wits' end. A co-worker had been pestering her to seek help before it got worse. The debt, the hopelessness, the anxiety, the sleepless nights, and the regrets were piling up and she was feeling the pain.

"I couldn't sleep last night," she said.

She didn't know where to turn. She knew God would never leave her, but she was still faced with the reality of her financial mess. She and her husband had already downsized to an apartment. The house was long gone. A gift from God in a nineteen-month-old baby made this couple into a family, but with it came additional responsibilities. She earned more than her husband, but her salary barely covered the rent and utilities. Her husband worked only during the school year. Each day brought forth additional debt and further worry.

I will not soon forget the time I heard a mortgage broker tell me debt was good and that everyone should have it. If he could only hear the broken heart on the other side of the telephone he might be freed from his prison of self-deception. The feelings are real, though, and the consequences of financial pain are visceral and they manifest themselves in physical ways.

According to an Associated Press-AOL Health Poll, when people are dealing with mountains of debt, they are much more likely to report health problems such as ulcers, severe depression, heart attacks, trouble concentrating, and sleeping, and are even more prone to get upset for no good reason.[71] Some ten to sixteen million people are "… suffering terribly due to their debts, and their health is likely to be negatively impacted," says Paul J. Lavrakas, a research psychologist and AP consultant who analyzed the results of the survey.

Susan knew the reasons and symptoms without an expert weighing in. She was experiencing the pain that seemed to never go away.

Many experience a temporary fix to their heartache by anesthetizing their pain and diverting their heart. A new purchase, "a new drug" of sorts, as Huey Lewis sang about in the '80s.

Susan had purchased a new car within the year to cope with the difficult economic times facing her family. Now she drove the new car without auto insurance—a very risky gamble, all because she did not have enough for the payment, the rising cost of fuel, and insurance.

She trusted God for salvation, but not really to help her maneuver her family's finances. True, they moved into an apartment but it was still more than they could afford. Her husband was off during the summer and lining up a job during that time was not a priority for him. They needed to take the next step—living below their means and trusting God to open the doors and provide for them in miraculous ways.

She surrendered the rest of her heart to God on the telephone. She was willing to get out of the boat and walk toward the outstretched hand of Christ and trust Him to never leave her nor forsake her.

The fear that had riveted her to remain in her overpriced apartment and drive a car she could not afford caused her to believe she was a prisoner.

It was a beautiful search and rescue, though. I consider it a taste of Heaven to watch this transformation take place time and time again in people's lives.

For all of you who are tired and weary and cannot go on any longer, Jesus sends you this message, "Tired, worn out, burned out on religion? Come with me and recover your life, learn the unforced rhythms of My grace." [72]

The forces against you will not prevail and the forces that hold you will not fail.

DAY 32

Armed, Dangerous, and Slinging Cement

"FROM THAT DAY ON, HALF OF MY MEN DID THE WORK, WHILE THE OTHER HALF WERE EQUIPPED WITH SPEARS, SHIELDS, BOWS, AND ARMOR ... THOSE WHO CARRIED MATERIALS DID THEIR WORK WITH ONE HAND AND HELD A WEAPON IN THE OTHER, AND EACH OF THE BUILDERS WORE HIS SWORD AT HIS SIDE AS HE WORKED." (NEHEMIAH 4:16-18)

"IT IS AN UNFORTUNATE HUMAN FAILING THAT A FULL POCKETBOOK OFTEN GROANS MORE LOUDLY THAN AN EMPTY STOMACH."
– FRANKLIN DELANO ROOSEVELT

"I HAVE NO MONEY, NO RESOURCES, NO HOPES. I AM THE HAPPIEST MAN ALIVE." – HENRY MILLER

The threat was not taken away. It was just extinguished until another day. We can live in fear of the next attack or work with a weapon in one hand and a tool in the other. True, this is not our first choice in pursuing the life of leisure and comfort. We are looking forward to the blessings of retirement: a pension and unhindered fun in Branson, Missouri, or Pigeon Forge, Tennessee.

The thought of the big boy's Winnebago, now upgraded to a $200 thousand tour bus equipped with satellite TV and Internet, and just maybe your own golf cart—now that's the life. John Piper, in his most eloquent and non-offensive way says, "This is a wasted life."[73]

What makes a group of people willing to work like these folks on the wall? They knew where they had come from and trusted the awesome God who brought them out.

Do you trust Him enough to work with a weapon in one hand and a tool in the other, ready to battle the evil one, repairing your financial fortress?

This is what it looks like. You have now been convinced that God's warnings against debt and consumption are not to hurt you but to free you. It is not what He wants *from* you; it's what He wants *for* you. You have had a family meeting and all hands are on deck and willing to work towards eliminating the debt, decreasing spending, and bringing in as much as possible. Through extra hours at work, Ebay, garage sales—whatever you can do, you'll do.

You have also chosen to downsize, to eliminate cable, and give yourself a maximum amount to spend on groceries, eating out, and entertainment. There are things, though, that you will be going without. You can start with the easy things like cable, a home phone (using a cheap cell line or none), getting rid of a car, or moving. They may not seem easy at the moment, but your financial fortress is at stake, and you have been chosen for such a time as this.[74]

Getting uncomfortable will either draw you closer to your God or drive you to take matters into your own hands. Nehemiah prayed and posted guards. The people rebuilding the city built with an eye on the vulnerable areas and worked with all their might.

When we decide to lean on our own understanding, we fear what could happen instead of fearing God. When we trust in Him, He will protect us.

Again, here is what it looks like. You have made the decision to go without life insurance, a second car, a telephone, air conditioning, putting money in a retirement fund, dental insurance, eating out, vacations, cable, Internet, and a glut of other "necessities" for six months. Your friends and family will think you're nuts, your mother-in-law will light candles for you, and your dog will hate you.

The first step is to commit this plan to God, and He will make it succeed if it this plan is to honor Him.

Here is the glue that holds this truth together: "Commit to the Lord whatever you do and your plans will succeed" (Proverbs 16:3). Your plan to do all of this can be tracked and followed on a spending plan. (To get a free, downloadable spending plan go to www.account417.com for a spending plan in Excel.)

Post the guards at the vulnerable places. How do we do this financially? Make a list of all of the areas that you are vulnerable—post-it notes are fine for those with limited patience. Remember all additional income and freed-up money goes on the current debts or short-term goals. When you are tempted to purchase, go back over the vulnerable list and ask yourself this question: "Will this help me achieve my goal or not?" If not, scrap it. If so, weigh it and determine if this so-called need or purchase will help to shore up a vulnerable area.

For example, you are convinced that your $3,800 per month mortgage is essential to your survival, and that you will never, ever get the chance to buy a home in this area again if you don't keep it, you would be a fool to get rid of it, and you really haven't lost *that* much on it or you have lost *too* much to get rid of it. It is time to take a deep breath, and trust that God has a better plan than a thirty-year prison sentence. A plan that includes a home equity line of credit or an interest-only mortgage that some fast-talking, profit-seeking mortgage broker told you would be crazy not to do? God does not want you to live this way.

Upgrade today. God wants to take this weight off your shoulders. Jesus actually says, "Come to me, all you who are ... burdened, and I will give you rest. Take my yoke upon you ... for my yoke is easy ... and enjoy the unforced rhythms of my grace."[75]

Maria was a single mom who was praying for a BMW. She did not care how much she had to sacrifice, how long she had to work extra jobs. She hated her Honda Civic. As a mother of two small children, one of them disabled, she needed more than a two-seater. God knew this, but she didn't know He did. Someone donated a van to us to give to a single mom. I knew just the one: Maria.

I called to see how she was doing and she said she was still praying for a BMW and God was already in the process of answering her prayers. She had totaled her Honda that day and she had started another part-time job. She was now working eighty hours per week.

She still knew God was going to bring her a BMW. She then asked to come speak to me about it. She got a ride and when she arrived, I saw the fatigue in her eyes and the heartache in her face because of not being able to spend time with her children. I knew God was not going to force His gifts on His unwilling children, but I knew I needed to point her to His Word.

The first place was in Luke 11, where Jesus' disciples asked Him how to pray. He said to pray for your daily bread.

I then asked Maria, "What would daily bread look like in your situation?"

She said a BMW. I asked why.

She said, "Everyone would think I was doing well if I drove a BMW."

I then directed her to the passage in Matthew 11:28-30. I asked her to close her eyes and think about the burden, the backpack with the rocks in it, that she was carrying around. Then I asked her to think about the most precious things in her life. With her eyes still closed she said her children and then she started to cry.

I then asked if this eighty-hour work schedule was bringing her pain or peace, and if her children would be happier with a BMW or more time with her. She wept bitterly. I asked her to give her burdens to the One whose burden is light and she did.

I then asked her to pray for bread. This time she asked God for whatever He had in store for her, because she trusted Him now.

In all my counseling with thousands of individuals and couples, I have never seen someone that broken. It was as if the weight of an actual car was lifted from her. I then opened my desk drawer and picked up a set of keys to a slightly used minivan, gave them to her and said, "This is God's gift to you, but He never forces His gifts on anyone." She cried even more. I then told her to tell her ride to leave. The evil one will use any opportunity to hold us back from God's incredible and life-bringing plan.

She thought briefly and said, "I have all of my things in his car. I can't... ."

I told her to get her things and I would help her to her new vehicle. She looked like Rocky Balboa after the fight, the make-up literally dripping off her face. Using multiple tissues had caused her eyes to swell and turn beet red.

When she saw the van for the first time, her face lit up and she smiled from ear to ear and said, "It's white."

I thought for a moment, "Oh, no, I only have one color!"

She then said, "I always wanted a white vehicle."

"God, you rock!"

She drove away and my faith in His great power grew.

So get rid of the house, even if you lose on it. Chances are you cannot afford it, or you could never afford it. This may be the best time in history to rent.

Keep track of what you owe and make payments. While thousands, perhaps millions, walk away without any thought of repaying, you will repay. The world will know your God is great when you do this. When people ask why, just tell them in your Code from Psalm 37:21, "The wicked borrow and do not repay, but the righteous give generously." Tell them you place the highest value on the ultimate treasure—Jesus Christ!

DAY 33

The Season of Sacrifice

"Neither I nor my brothers nor my men nor the guards with me took off our clothes; each had his weapon, even when he went for water." (Nehemiah 4:23)

"Whatever gain I had, I counted as loss for the sake of Christ. Indeed I count everything as loss because of the surpassing worth of knowing Christ Jesus as Lord." (Philippians 3:7-8)

"This is the season of sacrifice." – Stuart Easterly

Stuart Easterly is a great friend and in charge of stewardship at a large and effective church. Whenever I am in his town, he and I have the honor of coaching couples and individuals having financial difficulties or desiring some type of financial counsel. One of his favorite challenges to those we counsel is this phrase: "This is the season of sacrifice." I still remember the wide-eyed, eyebrow-raised, neck-stretched look of wonder and doubt from hundreds of faces upon hearing him deliver these words.

Nehemiah and the people were unfazed by this reality. They knew too much was riding on this call. They knew they could trust the God who had led them this far. They knew they were in the middle of something life-changing. They knew this was just a season, a season of sacrifice.

What about us? Can we get our heads around that concept? Or will we listen to the enemy and run and hide and spend until we have as much temporary satisfaction as we can go into debt for? All the while never experiencing the deep pleasure of being truly satisfied.

Today is the first day of the season of sacrifice for some, while others know this season all too well. Ask God right now to empower you to listen to His voice and not the voice of your family, your church, your friends, or your enemies. Listen to the Creator of the universe. He is waiting and will be with you every step during this season. You will not only make it through, but will receive treasures of great pleasure. That sounds like an oxymoron. It is hard to believe that joy can be found in suffering, but it can. It is called obedience and God rewards this.

When we place the greatest value on the ultimate treasure, there is nothing we keep off the table for God to use—from hobbies to houses, from classic cars to cameras, from retirement accounts to running gear, from organic foods to *Oriental Trading*, and everything in between.[76] If you really trust God, take your (actually, His) money, certain things like houses, time-shares, leased or financed cars, or whatever is precious to you to the altar, Abraham-style.[77]

Either He will rescue what you are willing to give up to obey Him and show Him that He is your treasure, or He will provide an even better substitute for what you have surrendered.

After the season of sacrifice, you will be a strong advocate for this life of simplicity. Many have decided they would continue living simply and find a more satisfying place to invest what has now been rescued from the unfulfilling life of consumption.

Nehemiah and his people knew this was a season of sacrifice. How about you? Do you have this kind of faith? You can.

DAY 34

Debt, Death, and Taxes

"SOME WERE SAYING, 'WE AND OUR SONS AND DAUGHTERS ARE
NUMEROUS; IN ORDER FOR US TO EAT AND STAY ALIVE, WE MUST GET
GRAIN.' OTHERS WERE SAYING, 'WE ARE MORTGAGING OUR FIELDS, OUR
VINEYARDS AND OUR HOMES TO GET GRAIN DURING THE FAMINE.' STILL
OTHERS WERE SAYING, 'WE HAVE HAD TO BORROW MONEY TO PAY THE
KING'S TAX ON OUR FIELDS AND VINEYARDS. ALTHOUGH WE ARE OF
THE SAME FLESH AND BLOOD AS OUR COUNTRYMEN AND THOUGH OUR
SONS ARE AS GOOD AS THEIRS, YET WE HAVE TO SUBJECT OUR SONS
AND DAUGHTERS TO SLAVERY. SOME OF OUR DAUGHTERS HAVE ALREADY
BEEN ENSLAVED, BUT WE ARE POWERLESS, BECAUSE OUR FIELDS AND
OUR VINEYARDS BELONG TO OTHERS.'"(NEHEMIAH 5:2-5)

"WILT THOU SEAL UP THE AVENUES OF ILL? PAY EVERY DEBT,
AS IF GOD WROTE THE BILL!" – RALPH WALDO EMERSON

"ONE MUST BE POOR TO KNOW THE LUXURY OF GIVING."
– GEORGE ELIOT

The enemy is within, the permanent resident in our hearts that is the DNA for all financial failure. It lies dormant until it is awakened by the stimulation of greed. Not many would use the word *greed* to describe their financial actions. Words like *savvy investments*, *moderate risk*, *growth positions*, and even *helping people* sound much more commendable.

But in Nehemiah's time, the day of full disclosure came screeching to a literal stop. The people could be attacked at any moment. They were threatened by an unknown enemy that lurked in the night; they were in danger and worked constantly to build up the exposed and vulnerable places behind their homes, and now, after about a month of this, the bills were due. The real world. You know, the Monday after the sermon that inspired you, the reality of your beliefs is put to the test.

Almost a thousand years after Nehemiah, men, women, children, and entire families in Ghana would be corralled like cattle, a thousand at a time. They were forced by merchants of greed to pass through a narrow doorway, never to return. Three million Africans were violently abducted—families experiencing each other's love, working and developing their skills together, living their lives. And then the great holocaust of the 1600's and 1700's occurred and they were herded through a single doorway that now reads: "Door of No Return." Not only in Ghana, but capturing countless souls from other abduction ports as well.

These profiteers sold human beings as machines. Human trafficking at its most elaborate and most organized. Opportunists from all corners of the globe cashed in on the financial gain. Many who called themselves "Christians."

How could a Christian force 1000 Africans into a hull of a ship and sell or buy other humans without considering Paul's words in a letter he wrote to the church in Philippi, "Do nothing out of selfish ambition or vain conceit, but in humility consider others better than yourselves. Each of you should look not only to your own interests, but also to the interests of others."[78a]

Are Christians immune to sin? No, unfortunately. Perhaps the most popular, yet most socially acceptable, sin in most Christian circles is greed. Greed is not good, but it ain't bad, so we harbor it in our hearts. This is what we have all heard: "We have to make a living."

"I am not a greedy person; I just like nice things."

"To be a Christ-kid I will name it and claim it and live with great abundance."

However, since the beginning of recorded history, the desire for money has an hallucinogenic effect on us and, as a result, has turned countless humans from the faith and pierced them with many a grief.

May the atrocities of the past never be forgotten, and, more importantly, may they never be repeated. This can only take place by being true followers of Christ. Education about slavery will remind us of our heinous crimes against humanity, but will not prevent new generations from similar sins.

The only remedy is to truly follow Christ and His example. He showed us the most basic way to live when He said, "Greater love has no one than this, that he lay down his life for his friends. You are my friends if you do what I command." There is a debt to pay to those who have been wronged—a debt that should never be paid off, and payments should be made daily. It is the debt to love one another more than ourselves. Let's start paying this enormous and very delinquent debt.[78b]

Nehemiah's people thought they were surviving. They did what they had to do in their own understanding of finance. This meant, "If I have something you need you can borrow it with interest. I need to survive too." This practice takes time-tested business principles and merges them into everyday, family life. The problem is that it leaves no room for faith and a God that honors such faith.

Nehemiah's people knew all too well about being treated as dollar-store items, and traded like baseball cards. Years earlier they were pardoned, bought back, and liberated from the tyranny of slavery.

But what happened next is a scheme only perfected by the evil one. Not one of Nehemiah's people would have condoned slavery when they were oppressed, but when faced with the opportunity to lend to their own brothers, and perhaps to make a meager profit, they opened the door to great opportunity for a familiar pain. After a short while *the have-nots* were in debt to *the haves*, and falling deeper into bondage.

It is your turn. With eyes wide open to where you are or where you are going, it is time to stop the train that is on the wrong track or has already derailed, and do it God's way financially. You do not have to be enslaved to the bondage of debt, greed, or any other lesser gods.

What to do next? See tomorrow ...

DAY 35

Greed Is the Absence of Trust in a Rich God

"I AND MY BROTHERS AND MY MEN ARE ALSO LENDING THE PEOPLE MONEY AND GRAIN. BUT LET THE EXACTING OF USURY STOP! GIVE BACK TO THEM IMMEDIATELY THEIR FIELDS, VINEYARDS, OLIVE GROVES AND HOUSES, AND ALSO THE USURY YOU ARE CHARGING THEM—THE HUNDREDTH PART OF THE MONEY, GRAIN, NEW WINE AND OIL. 'WE WILL GIVE IT BACK,' THEY SAID. 'AND WE WILL NOT DEMAND ANYTHING MORE FROM THEM. WE WILL DO AS YOU SAY... . '"(NEHEMIAH 5:10-12)

"A GREEDY FATHER HAS THIEVES FOR CHILDREN." – SERBIAN PROVERB

"THE EASIEST WAY FOR YOUR CHILDREN TO LEARN ABOUT MONEY IS FOR YOU NOT TO HAVE ANY." – KATHERINE WHITEHORN

What happens when we have egg on our faces? What if your failure is much worse than mine? Are you wrong and am I right? What if God reveals to us that we all have been tempted by greed? Simply put, greed is the absence of belief in a God who provides generously.

Think about it for a moment.

We get caught up in the refinance game, the allure of flipping property, investing in risky investments, or that *sure thing* that will double, even triple our holdings. We question that if we follow the biblical axioms such as slow and steady brings prosperity or "… he who gathers little by little makes it grow," in the old-school way, we will be seen as foolish.[79]

Nehemiah could either spin the blame on someone else, minimize his involvement in the greed scheme, or just face it, confess it, and make a statement and a law that would keep everyone honest, accountable, and fully aware of the pain of not managing finances God's way.

The Mosaic Law prescribed lending without interest to a fellow countryman, but charging foreigners since ideally they would come to town for profit. What should catch our eyes in verse 10 of Nehemiah 5 is the word *usury*. We think of this in terms of credit cards, check-cashing stores, even loan sharks, but in Nehemiah's time the "hundredth part" was 1 percent. To charge 1 percent per month would be considered usury.[80]

But it wasn't so much the charging of interest that was so wrong. It was their lack of faith in God's provision if they didn't take matters into their own hands. They felt that in order to survive, it was absolutely necessary to charge interest to even the poorest of people. Those people, of course, were working without pay on the city and they were the same ones who had formerly been enslaved and were now extremely poor. This was where they doubted God's promises.[81] This is where we doubt God, too.[82]

Josephus explains the Law and the spirit of the Law in Nehemiah's day: "Let it not be permitted to lend upon usury to any Hebrew either meat or drink; for it is not just to draw a revenue for the misfortunes of a fellow countryman. Rather, in consoling him in his distress, you should reckon as gain the gratitude of such persons and the recompense that God has in store for an act of generosity."[83]

The more benevolent they were, the less they would earn, and subsequently the less they would have for themselves. Therefore, human nature compels us to seek a profit even at someone else's expense, as the simple Maslow hierarchy of needs explains. But that is where we go wrong.

We default in our thinking and acting when we engage in the belief that "we will take it from here." Thus, trusting in

God to provide for us is a foolish decision. In Nehemiah's case he may not have been getting interest on his loans, but he was certainly not planning on writing off the debt. Interest-free is one extreme, but lending without expecting anything in return is just plain dumb. Here is what our hearts say, "If everyone did this we would all be broke."

Plain and simple, greed says that I cannot trust whoever or whatever my god is and must take matters into my own hands.[84] I must truly lean on my intellect, my abilities, and my power and do what I need to do to survive and thrive.

Nehemiah had experienced the power, provision, and pleasure of an intimate sweetness with God. Could he trust Him for what he was about to do? This was the first step.

God did not force it out of his hands. Nehemiah saw his lack of faith was exactly the same as the usury being charged by some of his people to one another. This enlarged Nehemiah's faith like no other single action in the area of finance. Had he not associated himself with those who were doing things even more abusive, he may not have considered exempting his people from tax, a move that could have proved to bankrupt this new city.

Nehemiah trusted God not only with his possessions and his ability to earn money, but he trusted the Provider to take care of him as he followed and listened to Him.

This single event changed Nehemiah's future financial goals forever and gave us a pattern to follow for generations. Now it is your turn. Nehemiah set the standard and it started with trusting God financially. He and his people stopped lending, loans that were outstanding were forgiven, and the interest charged given back. No financial book could or would ever be written endorsing these types of foolish financial techniques.

This entire book was inspired by the actions and change in Nehemiah's heart as recounted in Chapter 5 of his memoirs. These clear violations of the world's way of handling money either cause a contradiction or a confirmation of the wisdom of God's economy. Clearly throughout history man has tried it the world's way. The extent of this mindset has turned people into profit, and we have *used* people and *loved* money. God's way is just the opposite—use money to love people.

Nehemiah tapped into the love channel. Read my lips: "No more greed."

DAY 36

The Fair Tax

"... NEITHER I NOR MY BROTHERS ATE THE FOOD ALLOTTED TO THE
GOVERNOR. BUT THE EARLIER GOVERNORS—THOSE PRECEDING ME—
PLACED A HEAVY BURDEN ON THE PEOPLE AND TOOK FORTY SHEKELS OF
SILVER FROM THEM IN ADDITION TO FOOD AND WINE... ."
(NEHEMIAH 5:14-15)

"IT IS A KIND OF SPIRITUAL SNOBBERY THAT MAKES PEOPLE THINK THEY
CAN BE HAPPY WITHOUT MONEY." – ALBERT CAMUS

"HOW DO WE ENSURE THAT OUR HUMAN WORK HAS MORE THAN THE
LIFESPAN OF A SAND-CASTLE AT THE OCEAN'S EDGE?" – OS GUINNESS

Forty shekels add up to about a pound of silver. In today's monetary value, silver is around fifteen dollars an ounce and there are sixteen ounces in a pound, so that comes to $240 per person. That would pay for a great deal of the city's services. Nehemiah could have said, "People have no idea how much it takes to run a city government. I am not putting this money in my pocket; I am investing it in them."

That would certainly be a reasonable statement. But Nehemiah said neither. He decided to fund the part of the project that was unwritten by King Artaxerxes. This was much more than I am sure he expected. But he remembered the money-hungry men who preceded him and he would not even breathe like them. Their god was their stomach, but Nehemiah's God was the greatest of all treasures, and his citizenship was in Heaven.[85] [86]

The city was tax-free. If the people didn't pay for the public services, then who would? Nehemiah was willing to trust God to stretch his nest egg and foot the bill for this gigantic family. What he did not have, God would provide. He would not have been a good politician today. He certainly wouldn't make it on a corporate board; the stockholders would reject such a "Boy Scout." He would have made it on only a few church boards with his radical financial beliefs. Certainly the learned board members would attempt to groom him to become a bigger and better disciple through borrowing and bonds. But Nehemiah had a new focus, a new hunger for true riches, and a new desire for his eternal home. He was focused on life change; he was addicted to a God who satisfies.

Fifty-two days of this tax-free stuff is plausible, even commendable. It may have gotten him re-elected. But Nehemiah did this for twelve years. Nehemiah's faith was stretched daily. His dependence on himself was non-existent. His God was *big*.

What if our God gets this big? Could we trust Him as much as we trust ourselves? More?

We were remodeling the kitchen at the office. The handyman brought us a slightly used almond-colored dishwasher to use and we accepted the gift, but decided to use the one that was still operating. We had the almond-colored dishwasher in the hallway for weeks until we decided to set it outside for drive-by scavengers to pick up some evening. They did, and we were happy to unload it. After all, it was almond colored.

Every Thursday, we would close the tax and accounting practice and wear a different hat—the financial counselor hat.

Renee came in for an appointment one day. She was a single mom who I had not seen for a few months. She sheepishly revealed a new credit card bill, a Sears account with a balance of $555, at 18 percent interest and subject to higher APR. I asked what the story was. She said her dishwasher went out, and she really wanted a particular color and could not imagine such a foolish prayer to God. A request for a dishwasher, sure, but a particular color? No! Now that takes the cake.

Can you imagine every man, woman, and child in the world bothering God for the exact color of what they are asking for? What is He? The Sears Catalog? QVC? The Internet? No way, God ain't no vending machine. As C.S. Lewis said, "He is good, but He is not tame."[87] But does that mean you don't ask for a color and settle for whatever He wants to give you and you will like it or else? No, that is not what C.S. Lewis was saying.

Such a good God, coupled with the closeness of a best friend, results in a satisfying trust—a trust that knows whatever He provides is the best because He promises "… no good thing will I withhold from those whose walk is blameless."[88]

So whatever happened to Renee? When she mentioned she bought a dishwasher and had to charge it because she had no money and she wanted a certain color and God couldn't fill her order, I had to sheepishly ask the question, "You didn't happen to need an almond-colored dishwasher, did you?"

She said, "Yes, that is exactly the color I wanted!"

I told her how I was given a dishwasher that I didn't need and so I put it outside after some calls to folks that might have needed it. She said, "I thought about calling you, but I was embarrassed to ask for a certain color." I told her that dishwasher should have gone to her. She left knowing a bigger, more-loving God than she came in with. So can you.

DAY 37

The Secret to Riches!

"... THEIR ASSISTANTS ALSO LORDED IT OVER THE PEOPLE. BUT OUT OF REVERENCE FOR GOD I DID NOT ACT LIKE THAT. INSTEAD, I DEVOTED MYSELF TO THE WORK ON THE WALL. ALL MY MEN WERE ASSEMBLED THERE FOR THE WORK; WE DID NOT ACQUIRE ANY LAND."
(NEHEMIAH 5:15-16)

"OUR ONLY TROUBLE IS THAT WE HAVEN'T LAND ENOUGH. IF I HAD PLENTY OF LAND, I SHOULDN'T FEAR THE DEVIL HIMSELF."[89] – PAHÓM

"HIS SERVANT PICKED UP THE SPADE AND DUG A GRAVE LONG ENOUGH FOR PAHÓM TO LIE IN AND BURIED HIM IN IT. SIX FEET FROM HIS HEAD TO HIS HEELS WAS ALL HE NEEDED." [90] (THE FINAL WORDS OF *HOW MUCH LAND DOES A MAN NEED?* BY LEO TOLSTOY)

"OUR PASSION IS PLACING THE GREATEST VALUE ON THE ULTIMATE TREASURE." – ACCOUNT417.COM

What a loser. Nehemiah will never get ahead by missing these opportunities of a lifetime. His mother and father will not be able to say of him, "My son is doing so very well. He is the governor of a big city." No, their son-bragging would sound like this, "Our son is in ministry, worked for the king and was doing very well and now he is helping people. But he will do well again, someday; he's a good boy and such a hard worker. And he's so nice too." You see the difference. We are judged, measured, sized up, "atta–boyed," and bragged upon by how *well* we do. Nehemiah was filthy rich. Well, not exactly filthy, more like righteously rich. Somehow that just has a better ring to it.

Deep down inside, most of us believe that if you do not do well—the money, the earthly possessions, the land—you really are not successful. But what if God's idea of success is the polar opposite of the world's view? Nehemiah believed this with all of his heart. No other explanation could be given for the changes that took place in his heart and the actions that followed.

He came face-to-face with history repeating itself regarding slavery. He abolished slavery. He shared with a generosity that could not be repaid. He embraced giving without any possibility of being repaid and led by example to his own financial detriment. He then made the first public law, which was, interestingly, a financial law. The law stated that anything taken from a debtor would be given back to him or her, including houses, land, crops, and money plus the interest charged to them.

Not just giving them back what was held as collateral? No. Everything. Including the interest charged. Rewarding the debtors? It might seem so, but it was wiser than that. Debts were forgiven, second chances had been distributed, and a new law not to borrow was in place.

What was the penalty for a violation of this law? May God shake out of His house and possession every person that did not obey this law. Remarkably, not only those who were in debt favored such sudden economic freedom, but also everyone praised God for this oath, which they took.

Is it fair that those who borrowed did not have to repay? No. Was it right that those who loaned got stuck without their principle or any interest? No. Was this a way to fundraise? No. Was this a way to lift people? Oh, yes! When the source of our hope and survival is revealed and the result is something or someone other than God, we are forced to choose sides. Remain with the god who cannot see our pain or hear our cries for help, or upgrade to the God who is far more powerful than 1 percent per month—the amount they were charging each other for interest on money in Nehemiah's day.

Nehemiah knew he had been called to this royal position for such a time as this. Okay, so he is not Esther, who, roughly thirty years earlier, heard those exact words from her cousin Mordecai, just before she performed the most courageous act of her life.[91]

The evidence of a life that was completely convinced that Heaven was its home and people were its Master's love made Nehemiah a prisoner to the truth—land had no stronghold. He invested there, not here. He demonstrated the life Jesus Christ himself showcased and had recorded in duplicate form by both the former tax collector Levy in Matthew 6:19-34 and retold by Dr. Luke in his account from Luke 12:32-34.

> Do not be afraid little flock, for your Father has been pleased to give you the kingdom. Sell your possessions and give to the poor. Provide purses for yourselve that will not wear out, a treasure in heaven that will not be exhausted, where no thief comes near and no moth destroys. For where your treasure is, there your heart will be also.

Nehemiah showed the people by example how to choose true riches and take hold of the life that is truly life.[92] [93] Now it is your turn to invest heavily in where you are going to spend eternity. Right before Joshua died at the age of one hundred, he challenged the people in the same way that years earlier he had challenged them. They must choose one of their earthly gods or Almighty God who had brought them out of slavery, kept them safe, and given them land, food, and freedom.[94] They made a covenant to follow the one true God, and put a stone next to an oak to remind them daily of their sober commitment.

Today, get a rock or a paperweight and set it up on a shelf or a table and say to God that you will put your complete financial trust in Him, and, as in Joshua's day, say it out loud so that the rock or paperweight hears you. It may sound a little odd, but why not have a constant reminder in your home that stares at you every day as a reminder of the commitment you made and Who you made it to?

Email me and let me know what thing you used to remind you of your commitment at kevin@52days.com.

DAY 38

One More

"FURTHERMORE, A HUNDRED AND FIFTY JEWS AND OFFICIALS AT MY TABLE, AS WELL AS THOSE WHO CAME TO US FROM THE SURROUNDING NATIONS. EACH DAY ONE OX, SIX CHOICE SHEEP AND SOME POULTRY WERE PREPARED FOR ME, AND EVERY TEN DAYS AN ABUNDANT SUPPLY OF WINE OF ALL KINDS. IN SPITE OF ALL THIS, I NEVER DEMANDED THE FOOD ALLOTTED TO THE GOVERNOR, BECAUSE THE DEMANDS WERE HEAVY ON THESE PEOPLE." (NEHEMIAH 5:17-18)

"WHY SURE YOU CAN COME OVER FOR DINNER, WE'LL JUST PUT ANOTHER CUP OF WATER IN DA SOUP!" – SAID MARGIE FROM BISMARK

"IF THERE'S NO MONEY IN POETRY, NEITHER IS THERE POETRY IN MONEY." – ROBERT GRAVES

"OUR GOAL IS TO SHOW THE WORLD AND THE CHURCH THAT EVEN IN THESE LAST EVIL DAYS, GOD IS READY TO HELP, COMFORT, AND ANSWER THE PRAYERS OF THOSE WHO TRUST IN HIM. WE NEED NOT GO TO OUR FELLOWMEN OR TO THE WAYS OF THE WORLD. GOD IS BOTH ABLE AND WILLING TO SUPPLY US WITH ALL WE NEED IN HIS SERVICE."
– GEORGE MULLER

Imagine Christmas Eve, and you and your spouse are struggling students, with just soup as the main and only course. You get word that there are a few more student friends not going home for Christmas and will be your guests around the table. Wil and Nan, forty-five years as foreign missionaries and church planters, would just put another cup of water in the soup for each person who was coming to dinner.

That was then and this is now. We would just charge a few more bags of groceries at the local supermarket if that happened to us, but the faith of Nehemiah was much greater. Why? Because his God was bigger than ours.

He could have done the prudent financial thing of the day and collected a few carrots, squash, and chickens from the folks in the new town, but he knew it would be a financial hardship on them. So he dug deep into his own savings, his own pocket, his own security, and shared daily with many of them.

To whom much is given, much is expected. Nehemiah did not balk over this truth. Neither did he consider it a curse, but a great windfall. God had chosen wisely with Nehemiah who was a man whom He could trust with what had been entrusted to him. Nehemiah was a man who did not go the way of fear and the world, but placed his security in God. He could experience the truth of Jesus' words, "So if you have not been trustworthy in handling worldly wealth, who will trust you with the true riches?"[95]

Nehemiah chose the most secure route and the one with the greatest return on investment: people. Jesus revealed a deep truth about investing that Dr. Luke recorded hundreds of years later: "I tell you, use worldly wealth to gain friends for yourselves, so that when it is gone, you will be welcomed into eternal dwellings."[96] Nehemiah led the pace in the newly formed investment club by setting an example of radical-return investing. If merely securing the city was all that there was to be accomplished, that would not have been enough satisfaction beyond the fifty-two days. If accumulating more and more stuff as the governor was as good as it gets, that would have left him no better than the miserable tyrants he was battling because he was threatening their turf, their money. Nehemiah was changing the world by investing in people, not things.

His results? His rewards? Nehemiah spoke to God and said, "Remember me with favor, O my God, for all I have done for these people."[97] Nehemiah would not be disappointed. Jesus' words years later confirmed what Nehemiah believed of His God: that there would be people who were impacted by his sacrifice and would see that his God was good, not gold. They would know that his trust was not in his possessions, but that he was just passing through this life and every day he would seek to show others how great his God was.

What about you? Do you believe you are just passing through this life? Do you know that someday you will be face-to-face with God and you will have the chance to look back over your life and wonder what you could have invested more wisely? Perhaps pumping more into people than the tank, spending more on transporting the gospel than on cars would have had more eternal value?

One of the greatest reminders of all time of how short this life is and how urgent is the situation at hand is captured at the end of the movie, *Schindler's List*. This Spielberg film chronicles the life of Oscar Schindler, the German who spent the years of Hitler's war against the Jews, saving them by creating jobs in his munitions factory. Eleven hundred Jews were saved by Schindler's creative and courageous acts. However, at the end of the war, while all of the 1100 people surrounded him in a final farewell before going back to their lives, Oscar Schindler wept bitterly. He looked at his car and thought, "I could have saved ten more Jews," and then at his gold lapel pin and said, "I could have saved two more, at least one more." While he tried to speak through his sobs, he was comforted with the hugs of the people and the words of his accountant, his friend, and right hand, "There are 1100 people here because of you."

Oscar Schindler could not focus on the 1100 people he saved, although that was a miraculous feat. All he could think about were the ones that died a horrific and painful death at the hands of evil.

Nehemiah had no regrets about his investment strategy. You may not be able to change your past, but God wants to change your future so you finish well. Nehemiah's investment portfolio may not have included land or posh houses or condos or even a lot of money after buying meals for 600-800 people per day.[98] Today, for a typical restaurant to feed that many people with this amount of food would cost $3000. He did this every day. This comes to $156,000 for the fifty-two days. It also says he had wine delivered every ten days and that could easily double this amount.

Why would a guy spend his own money on meals for a restaurant full of people? Ask the thousands of people every day that share a meal or a bag of clothes with a homeless guy, or water and Powerbars with a woman on the street. Or ask the people who run soup kitchens all across America, day in and day out without fanfare, but who experience the sweet smiles of the appreciative recipients for life's basic need—food. Perhaps we have it all wrong. Perhaps giving *is* joyful and soul satisfying.

DAY 39

What Is Right Is Also Smart

" ... SHOULDN'T YOU WALK IN THE FEAR OF OUR GOD TO AVOID THE
REPROACH OF OUR GENTILE ENEMIES?" (NEHEMIAH 5:9)

"THE SAFEST WAY TO DOUBLE YOUR MONEY IS TO FOLD IT OVER AND
PUT IT IN YOUR POCKET." – KIN HUBBARD

"IF YOU MAKE MONEY YOUR GOD, IT WILL PLAGUE YOU LIKE THE DEVIL."
– HENRY FIELDING

Could it be that the correct thing to do is also the smart thing to do? Doing it God's way in Nehemiah's case meant avoiding being a hypocrite. There are things Nehemiah could have done as a governor that no one would have known, except God.

He wants us to be men and women who do not add validity to yet another pastor who arrives on the scene to promote a message that will make him or her rich. Should the life-changing message of Christ be used to merely make money? Paul spoke directly to this in his second letter to a church in Greece by the name of Corinth. He told them we do not, in fact, peddle God's Word for profit.

There are more needs today than at any other time in history. There is also an unprecedented amount of wealth being wasted. Hitting closer to home, those who say they are "Christ-followers" throughout the world control more wealth today than at any other time in history, to the tune of 16.4 trillion dollars in 2007.[99]

Yet *The 10/40 Window* [100] reveals 70 percent of the population in this area of the world does not know Jesus Christ. Half of the population lives on two dollars a day or less. We in America spend more each year on ice cream than what it would take to provide clean water, health care, and sanitation to the entire world. We will spend forty billion dollars this year on our pets. That comes out to $1,200 per year for each pet owner. The average giving family will contribute only $300 a year to send the life-changing message of Jesus Christ to those who are lost.

There is a disconnect. The problem is, duty and need are not enough to get people motivated. There has to be a deeper hook. Needs have only a certain guilt-producing draw for our wallets. What if there was something more satisfying linked to meeting someone's needs? Would that make a difference? According to a Harvard study, satisfaction goes up with giving. This is no new news to those who have read the promises of reward in the gospels.

But what if handling our finances God's way will not only take care of others but also fill us with pleasure—let's use the word *joy* for those who are unaccustomed to pleasure—knowing that He will absolutely take care of us so that we do not need to compromise and walk the line of hypocrisy. Thus, our neighbors, who may not be followers of Christ, will not say, "What freaks and fakes those Christians are." Instead they will say, "I have to hand it to those Christ-followers; they practice what they preach and it's true."

That is what Nehemiah was saying to himself and the people. That is what he is saying to us today too.

DAY 40

Why Are We Doing
What We Are Doing?

"THE WHOLE ASSEMBLY RESPONDED, "AMEN," AND THEY
PRAISED THE LORD... ." (NEHEMIAH 5:13, NLT).

"THE CHIEF REASONS FOR ESTABLISHING AN ORPHAN HOUSE ARE:
ONE, THAT GOD MAY BE GLORIFIED SHOULD HE BE PLEASED TO
FURNISH ME WITH THE MEANS IN ITS BEING SEEN THAT IT IS NOT IN VAIN
TO TRUST HIM, AND THAT THUS THE FAITH OF HIS CHILDREN MAY BE
STRENGTHENED. SECOND, THE SPIRITUAL WELFARE OF THE FATHERLESS
AND MOTHERLESS CHILDREN, AND THREE, THEIR TEMPORAL WELFARE."
– GEORGE MULLER

"A BANK IS A PLACE WHERE THEY LEND YOU AN UMBRELLA IN FAIR
WEATHER AND ASK FOR IT BACK WHEN IT BEGINS TO RAIN."
– ROBERT FROST

George Muller depended totally on God when he didn't have enough food for the orphans in his charge, as he wrote in his journal: "December 1, 1842: Someone may ask, 'Why don't you buy the bread on credit? What does it matter whether you pay immediately for it or at the end of the month?' My reply is this: If this work is the work of God, then He is surely able and willing to provide for it. He will not necessarily provide at the time we think that there is need. But when there is real need, He will not fail us. We may and should trust in the Lord to supply us with what we require at present, so that there may be no reason to go into debt. I could buy a considerable amount of goods on credit, but the next time we were in need, I would turn to further credit instead of turning to the Lord. Faith, which is maintained and strengthened only by exercise, would become weaker and weaker. At last, I would probably find myself deeply in debt with no prospect of getting out of it." [101]

God took care of George Muller as He did Nehemiah. Nehemiah was reminded of the fact that God was in control and that He operates outside our petty earthly logic and economics. Nehemiah's building of the fortress was not the primary goal. God could have done something miraculous and the walls would have appeared, or He could have put a hedge of angels around the city, which would have been certainly stronger and more daunting than a wall. But God wanted Nehemiah to exercise his faith muscles since they grow weak without vigilant use.

As Nehemiah obeyed and trusted God, all those around him did not think Nehemiah was the Lord, but that their God was incredibly powerful and His love was unconditional, even when they turned their backs on Him. What Nehemiah was finding out quickly was what George Muller wrote about when taking care of the orphans. It was not about the orphans being fed. That was third on the list of importance. First and foremost was that, as God provided in miraculous ways for His endeavor, Muller's trust deepened, the faith of those who participated in the miracles deepened, the kids were fed, and everyone experienced God's power. What a formula—God glorified, needs provided for, faith strengthened, and everyone fed, clothed, and housed.

Nehemiah experienced this same formula. God was glorified first and foremost, the scattered people of Israel unified, and the fortress completed in fifty-two days.

You may be asking this question: "I thought the goal was to build *my* financial fortress in fifty-two days?" You would be right, but that is not the whole goal. Building a fortress without anything to protect it can be likened to a Hollywood movie set. It appears whole when you stand in front of it, but upon further inspection, it has no depth and is held up by the most tenuous of supports. Such a structure would collapse with the slightest nudge.

When it is all complete, the financial fortress, however deep and beautiful, will not be the greatest accomplishment. Your deepened faith in Almighty God will be. Your faith will allow your heart to rest in Him no matter what the circumstances. You will have learned the secret of being content.[102]

As George Muller wrote in his autobiography, "Faith rests on the written Word of God, but there is no promise that He will pay our debts. The Word says, 'Owe no man any thing' (Romans 13:8). The promise is given to His children, 'I will never leave thee, nor forsake thee' (Hebrews 13:5). 'He that believeth on Him shall not be confounded' (I Peter 2:6). We have not scriptural grounds to go into debt."

Our goal is to show the world and the Church that even in these last evil days, God is ready to help, comfort, and answer the prayers of those who trust in Him. We need not go to our fellow men or to the ways of the world. God is both able and willing to supply us with all we need in His service."

DAY 41

Deferred Assets

"I ALSO DEVOTED MYSELF TO WORKING ON THE WALL AND REFUSED TO ACQUIRE ANY LAND... ." (NEHEMIAH 5:16, NLT)

"I'M TIRED OF LOVE; I'M STILL MORE TIRED OF RHYME; BUT MONEY GIVES ME PLEASURE ALL THE TIME." – HILAIRE BELLOC

"I'M SO POOR I CAN'T EVEN PAY ATTENTION." – RON KITTLE

Yes, deferred assets—it's a familiar financial term to those who are shrewdly looking to the future for benefit. Call it money in the bank without the risk. As a matter of fact, this investment strategy of Nehemiah was ingenious. We, too, can implement this easy yet lucrative plan to greater heights, deeper riches, and larger profits.

Nehemiah made a conscious decision to postpone a small fortune for a larger one. Not really rocket science, but noteworthy nonetheless. Any somewhat intelligent bloke, when faced with an easy investment question, would, of course, choose the big money, not the ham sandwich. Nehemiah chose a foolish path, humanly speaking, yet a brilliant maneuver eternally. He chose to forego the privileges of his position and love people over profit.

On November 2, 1841, George Muller wrote in his diary these words, "At the time of our great poverty, one pound was sent by a lady from Birmingham. [103] About half an hour later, I received ten pounds from a brother who had saved up one hundred and fifty pounds. He put it into a savings bank, but he now sees that to devote this money to the work of God glorifies the name of Jesus more than to keep it in the savings bank for a time of sickness or old age. If such times come, the same Lord who has cared for him in health and strength will also care for him then." George Muller's faith was so strong that he could state these words in his journal, but most importantly he lived them.

The Bible states: "Lay not up for yourselves treasures upon earth, where moth and rust doth corrupt, and where thieves break through and steal: But lay up for yourselves treasures in heaven, where neither moth nor rust doth corrupt, and where thieves do not break through nor steal: for where your treasure is, there will your heart be also" (Matthew 6:19-21, KJV).

This is a word for poor believers as well as for rich believers. It may be said, "But every prudent person seeks to increase his wealth that he may have plenty to leave his children or to have something for old age or for the time of sickness." This is the custom of the world. But we disciples of the Lord Jesus have been promised "... an inheritance incorruptible, and undefiled, and that fadeth not away" (1 Peter 1:4, KJV). If we seek, like the people of the world, to increase our possessions, those who are not believers may question whether we believe what we say about our inheritance and our heavenly calling.

Our Lord says that the Earth is a place "... where moth and rust doth corrupt, and where thieves break through and steal." All that is of the Earth, and in any way connected with it, is subject to corruption, change, and dissolution. No reality or substance exists in anything but heavenly things. Often the careful amassing of earthly possessions ends in losing them in a moment by fire, robbery, or a change in the world markets. In a little while, we all must leave this Earth, or the Lord Jesus will return. What use will earthly possessions be then?

Our Lord, however, does not merely tell us not to lay up treasure on Earth. If He had said no more on the subject, people might abuse this commandment and use it as an excuse to encourage extravagant habits, spending everything they have or can obtain on themselves. Jesus does not mean that we should live up to our income. He adds, "But lay up for yourselves treasures in heaven." Every penny given for the Lord's sake to poor brethren or to the work of God is a treasure laid up in our accounts in Heaven. When we go to Heaven, we go to the place where our treasures are and we shall find them there.

The Lord concludes: "For where your treasure is, there will your heart be also." Where should the heart of the disciple of the Lord Jesus be, but in Heaven? Our calling is a heavenly calling, our inheritance is a heavenly inheritance, and our citizenship is in Heaven. But if we believers in the Lord Jesus lay up treasures on Earth, then our hearts will be on Earth. Laying up treasures in Heaven will draw the heart heavenward. It brings along with it, even in this life, precious spiritual blessings as a reward of obedience to the commandment of our Lord.

Nehemiah tapped into the deferred riches at least three times in his restoration journey. First, he was faced with the economic uncertainty of not getting paid or supported while on his lengthy leave of absence. Going to the boss and asking for a leave of absence *with* pay and one *without* pay will, in most cases, determine whether it is granted.

What are you willing to postpone and trust God for until you achieve the return on your investment?

DAY 42

Homeland Security

"WHEN WORD CAME TO SANBALLAT, TOBIAH, GESHAM THE ARAB AND THE REST OF OUR ENEMIES THAT I HAD REBUILT THE WALL AND NOT A GAP WAS LEFT IN IT—THOUGH UP TO THAT TIME I HAD NOT SET THE DOORS IN THE GATES... ." (NEHEMIAH 6:1)

"LET NO DEBT REMAIN OUTSTANDING EXCEPT THE CONTINUING DEBT TO LOVE ONE ANOTHER." (ROMANS 13:8)

"FOR THE LORD YOUR GOD WILL BLESS YOU AS HE HAS PROMISED, AND YOU WILL LEND TO MANY NATIONS BUT WILL BORROW FROM NONE. YOU WILL RULE OVER MANY NATIONS BUT NONE WILL RULE OVER YOU." (DEUTERONOMY 15:6)

"TWO THINGS I ASK OF YOU, O LORD; DO NOT REFUSE ME BEFORE I DIE: KEEP FALSEHOOD AND LIES FAR FROM ME; GIVE ME NEITHER POVERTY NOR RICHES, BUT GIVE ME ONLY MY DAILY BREAD. OTHERWISE, I MAY HAVE TOO MUCH AND DISOWN YOU AND SAY, 'WHO IS THE LORD?' OR I MAY BECOME POOR AND STEAL, AND SO DISHONOR THE NAME OF MY GOD."(PROVERBS 30:7-9)

The city was still vulnerable, no matter how much work was completed. It was not time to rest. It was time to draw upon that eternal source of strength, the God of Nehemiah. It was time to make it.

There are two little cancers running amuck in our financial body that need to be eliminated and forever barred: debt and affluence. These are the two big culprits today and they have been around for all time. Nearly 3,000 years ago a wise man by the name of Agur echoed this truth when he penned the words, "… give me neither poverty nor riches."[104]

Debt is a cancer I have unfortunately seen and counseled against for over twenty years, often given refuge in the homes of many families. "Just a little debt," is what I've heard; but what I end up seeing is that the debt remains, fat and happy. Then at the end of many years the savings, the financial goals, the dreams, and the opportunities to change the world are gone.

There are defenders of debt. They are misguided and deceived individuals who believe it is just fine to toy with debt, believing that the amount of interest paid to credit card companies, or other creditors would just be squandered anyway.

There is a great illustration of the reality and the magnitude of us saying "Uncle" to debt. A financial planner in Naples, Florida, who goes by the name of Dutch, shows his clients how much money they would have at retirement if they had invested the $1,000 their granny gave them for graduation at seventeen years of age. If they put it in the bank at 3 percent and get the free toaster for opening an account, they would have a respectable $4,000 at the end. If they happen upon a 6 percent CD they would have a handsome $16,000 at the end. If they outperform the market and yield a coveted 12 percent return on investment they will have a whopping $256,000. If they are lucky and shrewd, maybe they could gain 18 percent on their $1,000, which would yield an incredible $4,096,000. Then he reveals the truth that lenders know all too well: 6 percent is gained routinely by mortgage companies, 12 percent gained by automobile financing companies, and 18 percent easily gained by credit card companies.

Impossible to *earn* 18 percent perhaps, but you are willing to *pay* 18 percent so that the credit card company can earn it? Think about the amount of money you could inject into missions. The average giving family gives approximately $25 per month to spread the life-changing message of Christ outside our borders. That is $300 per year.[105]

The average pet owner spends approximately $1,200 a year on Fido, a $40.8 billion (with a "B") per year industry compared to the $39 million (with an "M") given by all the average giving families.[106] It is a telltale sign of what has become really important. The sheer pleasure of seeing people move from an eternal death to welcoming me into their eternal homes is a whole lot more satisfying.[107]

Affluence is that comfortable state of waking up every morning with the ability to indulge in the next socially accepted, moral thing that sucks up your resources—resources that could be used to produce greater pleasure if done God's way.

I know what some of you are thinking: "You are saying God doesn't want me to have fun, or enjoy my blessings … ."

No, that's not it at all. He actually gave us all things to enjoy, as Paul wrote in a letter to a young pastor named Timothy. He wrote to this young pastor and said (in my best paraphrase): "Tell the folks in your church, 'Congratulations, you're rich; you may not feel rich compared to others who you're trying to keep up with, but your money and your stuff is going to let you down. God won't. Now transfer that trust from things to Him, who gave them to you in the first place to enjoy and to be rich. But not rich in today's definition; rich in doing cool stuff for people, selfless things, so people ask, where you came from. Don't stop there because I [God] am going to take care of you. Share what you have and your money with those who have needs. Now this is the really cool part. Not only are these people going to be taken care of, but God has a great reward for you to boot! Can you imagine having fun in sharing and not putting your hope in possessions? Plus there's a secret reward designed by the God who made the most beautiful things and pleasures on the planet. That's not all; there is more. People's lives will change and their hearts will be moved to accept me [Jesus Christ] as their Savior. We will all be high-fiving in Heaven, enjoying the

sweetest return on investment our hearts have ever dreamt up!"
(I Tim 6:17-19)

Drop the debt and ignore the urge to spend or hoard, and invest heavily where the greatest returns on investment lie.

DAY 43

Oh, No, *or Ono?*

"Sanballat and Gesham sent me this message: 'Come let us meet together in one of the villages on the plain of Ono.' But they were scheming to harm me... ." (Nehemiah 6:2).

"A zealous sense of mission is only possible where there is opposition to it." – D. W. Ewing

"Greed is all right; by the way I think greed is healthy. You can be greedy and still feel good about yourself." – Ivan F. Boesky

As if Nehemiah needed more trouble. Two out of the three stooges were at it again. They sent him a FedEx five times in row. They wanted him to stop the project and just talk to them about what was up and to give them a chance to explain things. True, they had plotted to kill him and overthrow the people, they had mocked him, ridiculed him, and were even anti-Semitic, but this time they just wanted to be friends and meet at Starbucks across town in a neutral location over tall, double-caramel macchiatos. They couldn't imagine Nehemiah saying no.

He did. He was focused on finishing. There were many lives hanging in the balance that were depending on him.

He saw through their deception. He sent this response: "... I am carrying on a great project and cannot go down. Why should the work stop while I leave it and go down to you?"[108]

Are you looking for a reason to stop? A great deal on a vacation, an interest-free credit card, a low mortgage rate, a bargain you cannot live without? Nehemiah knew this was not the time to shop or chitchat. It was time to finish strong and not allow any hurdles to be thrown into the financial mix by the enemy.

The evil one knows your soft spots. He knows what turns your head: the mall, the emails, the Internet, the mail, the dollar store. You actually know, too. It is not time for a diversion; it is time for focus.

You will be told, "You deserve it," "You've earned it," "You worked hard for it," "It's yours." Don't go to the plain of Ono. But maybe you are thinking right now, "I can't live like this forever!" so you will take this moment to check out of this financial fortress building and release a little steam, and then, after no harm is done, you will just go back and finish.

Beware of the cunning deception of your enemy. You cannot abandon your financial fortress while you build it up. That is what you are faced with, that is what has happened in the past.

This time will be different. You can make it. You are almost there. Don't stop. Focus on the goal, focus on the reward, focus on the celebration you will have upon completion of the milestones along the journey. For example, have something to look forward to when paying off a credit card or making great progress on another debt. Having something tangible to look forward to will make it easier during this 'season of sacrifice.' Plan low-cost fun now so when you achieve milestones you can record the date and the place you celebrated. Perhaps you will go to your favorite restaurant for paying off a certain amount of debt or eliminating a credit card that has had a balance for as long as you can remember. This time the food and the memory will be so much sweeter than the times when you were in debt and eating out was no big deal.

Celebration? We do that as followers of Christ? Oh, yeah, like no other partying ever. I am talking about all the pleasure without the guilt, pain, and heartache that is negotiated with every purchase of the world's deal.

Make a list of all of the weak spots you have and keep them front and center on the fridge. When the message comes, you will see that the evil one has no new tricks to deceive you with; they're just his old standbys. Give the list to a friend or a family member and ask them to call or email you periodically to check out how you are doing. This will draw the two of you closer and cause that person to evaluate areas in his or her life that may be susceptible to the enemy.

Here are a few "Ono's" that the evil one will bombard you with multiple times until you relent and give in:

Autos

The advertisements will be daily, not just once a day, but multiple times per day. Television, billboards, magazines, newspapers, radio, email, Internet, and direct mail will all try to get to you. You will not be able to stop them and eventually something they say will make you think you need a new car. In most cases the used car you have, that you have been taught to hate, is costing much less than a new car payment, not to mention the associated additional costs.

Credit Cards

They are perhaps even more aggressive than the automobile companies and more profitable. Refrain unless you are juggling from a higher interest rate to a much lower rate and you would be paying much more on that debt as a result.

Entertainment and Miscellaneous

This little culprit is responsible for consuming what little the family has left to live on or the amount that could be invested in the life-change of others. Give yourselves an allowance and put it in cash if you cannot resist using plastic. Don't squander the savings, though. This is easy to do. I cut my hair for an entire year to save the ten to fifteen dollars, but I did not put the money away in any type of account or envelope so that money was just spent on something else. So I went a whole year with ugly hair (since I had no idea what I was doing) and had nothing to show for it. The next year I got a little smarter. If I was to have bad haircuts, I was going show people why I had such a bad haircut with the cash in an envelope. This helped my self-image quite a bit.

DAY 44

The Smoking Gun

" ... IN HIS HAND WAS AN UNSEALED LETTER... ." (NEHEMIAH 6:5)

"MONEY FREES YOU FROM DOING THINGS YOU DISLIKE. SINCE I DISLIKE DOING NEARLY EVERYTHING, MONEY IS HANDY." – GROUCHO MARX

"A WISE MAN SHOULD ORDER HIS INTERESTS, AND SET THEM ALL IN THEIR PROPER PLACES. THIS ORDER IS OFTEN TROUBLED BY GREED, WHICH PUTS US UPON PURSUING SO MANY THINGS AT ONCE THAT, IN EAGERNESS FOR MATTERS OF LESS CONSIDERATION, WE GRASP AT TRIFLES, AND LET GO THINGS OF GREATER VALUE."
– FRANÇOIS, DUC DE LA ROCHEFOUCAULD

This is the bit of incriminating evidence that will destroy the entire project—the Watergate leak, the dress, the glove, the "unsealed letter." All have the potential to take down an entire movement. Truth should prevail, right? But what if it doesn't? Could a guilty man go free, while an innocent man is jailed? What about a plan that is so sinister that it will blow you out of the water, get you fired, arrested, and maybe killed; and here is the kicker—you are completely innocent and a target of jealous or just plain evil people? Nehemiah knows this situation all too well.

Here's the deal. The three stooges were up to their old tricks once again. Since Nehemiah was so focused on his fortress, each time he received a message to meet these jokers, he declined. They came up with a brilliant scheme that could just take care of everything. Write a letter that says that Nehemiah was secretly setting himself up to be king. Artaxerxes would have some competition and not just any competition, but from one of his own. It would be someone whom the king trusted. It reeked of betrayal and backstabbing toward the only person who believed in Nehemiah's mission. The wounds of a friend cut to the bone.

Not only was the plan to write the letter and send it by way of the king, but leaving it unsealed was brilliant. Because then at each stop when the message was transferred, curious eyes would feast upon the terrible words that exposed this do-gooder in sheep's clothing. In fact, the letter even stated that the three stooges were trying to talk this madman out of a death wish. When the king hears about this he will burn with such anger that all of the people in Jerusalem will experience the extent of his wrath.

What do you do? It's not true, but it could still ruin your life. Do you take matters into your own hands? Do you come down and fight on their level now? Do you stop everything you're doing and battle it? Or do you do what Nehemiah did and send a level-headed reply and stay on course?

Well, if you are like me, you stop everything you are doing and the world stands still. I fight a battle I was not created to deal with. Completing my task seems subordinate to the fight. Whatever rabbit hole the enemy has dug, I am now drawn into. The battle is already won by the enemy who has lured me with smoke and mirrors, and I have given up the place where I should be. Only to find out later that it was just a diversion to stop what I was doing and convince me to focus elsewhere.

All of us have a fight we were created for—one that we go head to head and hand to hand in combat with. Yet most of us take it to the streets, the public squares, the telephones, and not to the ring where the fight is actually won. God has designed each of us to be moved by something so heart-wrenching, tear-jerking, and people-saving, that if we were blessed with unlimited time, resources, and energy, we would literally be an army of one for life change.

Nehemiah was fully engaged in the battle of his life, and he was not going to allow the enemies of a great life change to derail him.

Was he worried? Did he take matters into his own hands? Did he move off base, fight a fight that wasn't his? No. He focused on the battle. His battle.

What is your battle? You've got one, don't you? I am not talking about the job of complaining and fighting the system, work, your spouse, your kids, the telephone company, the IRS, the school board, the company, the church, or the people that make you angry. I am talking about the battle that you were created to win. The others are diversions to sidetrack and get you to forget the main event. Nehemiah stayed focused and won the main event. God fought the main battle and the peripheral battles and got all of the credit at the end of the fifty-two days. Nehemiah and his people got the pleasure. That is God's recipe for our lives, " ... sorrowful, yet always rejoicing; poor, yet making many rich; having nothing, and yet possessing everything."[109]

Fight the good fight!

DAY 45

Remember Me, God?

"REMEMBER, O MY GOD, ALL THAT I HAVE DONE FOR THESE PEOPLE, AND BLESS ME FOR IT." (NEHEMIAH 5:19, NLT)

"AVARICE IS GENERALLY THE LAST PASSION OF THOSE LIVES OF WHICH THE FIRST PART HAS BEEN SQUANDERED IN PLEASURE, AND THE SECOND DEVOTED TO AMBITION. HE THAT SINKS UNDER THE FATIGUE OF GETTING WEALTH, LULLS HIS AGE WITH THE MILDER BUSINESS OF SAVING IT."
– SAMUEL JOHNSON

"... I OWE MY SOUL TO THE COMPANY STORE."
"18 TONS," SUNG BY TENNESSEE ERNIE FORD

"Hey, God, you remember me? I am the guy who did all of those things for others, putting myself last, and these backstabbing, jealous, mean-spirited, no-good jerks have been trying to put a serious hurtin' on me and I just want to make sure you remember all of this. Thanks, over and out, Nehemiah." Those would have been my words to God, in an honest attempt to rat out some weasels. If you are honest with yourself, your thoughts, and your heart, you have felt this way too.

You remember the time you were taken advantage of, or your heart was crushed by something incredibly insensitive, or you were let down by someone you loved and who said they loved you? Well, you are beginning to understand the fifty-two days that Nehemiah was having. He found himself the self-proclaimed governor of a broken-down community. He had papers from the king to prove it, but those papers didn't seem quite as important right about now.

You know exactly where he was. You and I have been there many times. Maybe even today. Our lives read like this: "Yet another difficult position I have been backed into and I see no way out of except by charging, borrowing, or indulging. I will have to do what I have to do."

Judy K is a single mom. She was caught up in the real estate debacle of the mid-2000's. She tried her hand at being a realtor and started making money, more than she had made in her whole life. With the increased earnings came increased spending. The only problem was that she spent tomorrow's dollars today. She bought this, that, and everything.

One of the items she purchased was an overpriced SUV that she felt she needed to show people that she was successful when she drove potential customers around. Because of less-than-perfect credit, the car set her back $1,000 per month. She dealt with it and anticipated the market continuing strong much, much longer. The market slowed, the leads dried up, and the golden days of fat paychecks were but a memory.

After hanging in there and piling on more and more debt, she knew she needed a job. A local church was hiring and she filled an administrative role. The pay was only $1,500 take-home per month. She was at her wits' end when she came to me for financial counsel. I asked her how big her God was. She said very big. I told her it was time to give up the SUV. She broke down like an old Pinto on the side of the road. The tears flowed. She said, "How will I get to work?" I asked again how big her God was, and she said between sobs, "My God is big!" She said later that if she hadn't cried so much she would have thrown up. Her God was big.

Her biggest fear was not having a car to get to work. What little income she earned could disappear if she couldn't get to her job. Her daughter then would not be supported and she would not be able to buy groceries; the worst fears a woman could face flashed before her eyes. She decided this time she would not try so much to rescue God, as she had done in the past. She would trust God up to the eleventh hour and then if He did not respond in her timing, she would lean on her own understanding and charge or borrow.

She reported three miracles to me.

She quickly called the company that financed her SUV and told them that she would have to give the car back. She asked if she sold the car to CarMax, would they accept that amount, which was far below what she owed them? Amazingly, they said yes. Miracle #1!

Next she asked the ladies at work to pray with her about a car, any car. She would be without a car in a matter of days. She was going to honor God and the finance company by giving the car back now instead of not making payments for three or four months and forcing them to repossess the car and incur additional costs that could be avoided.

True, she would owe the difference between what CarMax gave her and the loan balance, but she was committed to pay that difference as fast as she could.

Someone at work heard about the prayer for a car and offered her a car to use—Miracle #2! But behind every miracle is the evil one pleading with us to reconsider complete faith in Christ. The evil one always lies in wait at the eleventh hour and on the heels of victory.

Judy K wondered if she would ever get a car, and feared wearing out her welcome with the loaner. She thought she might lose her job if she kept the car longer then was reasonable. This placed great fear and anxiety in her mind and heart. Then she remembered the very words she had spoken—"My God is big!" She went to work trusting God. She then heard a local ministry, Sheridan House, occasionally receives cars for single moms and she decided to call and inquire. They said they didn't have one available, but they would let her know if one became available.

That sinking feeling of "What did I do?" finally hit her like a ton of bricks. The reality of God's timing versus our timing was so real she could touch it. The evil one would not win this battle, though. Her faith had been deepened. She thought, "That's okay; I will wait for God's timing." This little glimpse of her heart proved to be a crack in the heavens. What happened next was nothing less than living on the edge of the miraculous.

Miracle #3.

The person on the other end of the line said, "Hold on, Judy, someone is calling right now on the other line and is donating a car for a single mom." If Judy K did not have a strong heart we would never know this story. She was overwhelmed. When she picked up the car, she cried once again because God had not only given her a car for free, but the make, model, and color were the same as a car she had when she moved to the state. God got all of Judy K's heart during this process and now she is bringing people to the place where she works and goes to church. She cannot contain herself!

Living on the edge of the miraculous is a choice. Will you worship a big God or a small one?

DAY 46

The Gift of the Magi
(O. Henry's Classic Christmas Story)

"YET I REFUSED TO CLAIM THE GOVERNOR'S FOOD ALLOWANCE BECAUSE
THE PEOPLE WERE ALREADY HAVING A DIFFICULT TIME."
(NEHEMIAH 5:18B, NLT)

"GREED IS A BOTTOMLESS PIT WHICH EXHAUSTS THE PERSON IN AN
ENDLESS EFFORT TO SATISFY THE NEED WITHOUT EVER REACHING
SATISFACTION." – ERICH FROMM

"MY HEAVEN IS TO PLEASE GOD, AND GLORIFY HIM, AND TO GIVE ALL TO
HIM, AND TO BE WHOLLY DEVOTED TO HIS GLORY: THAT IS THE HEAVEN
I LONG FOR; THAT IS MY RELIGION, AND THAT IS MY HAPPINESS, AND
ALWAYS WAS EVER SINCE I SUPPOSE I HAD ANY TRUE RELIGION: AND
ALL THOSE THAT ARE OF THAT RELIGION SHALL MEET ME IN HEAVEN."
– DAVID BRAINERD.

Maybe the stakes are higher than a new car. Maybe you are facing being homeless, and you wish it were just a matter of transportation. Anyone can trust God for a car, but a house is a whole lot different. Right? Tell that to Rain. She, too, was a single mom with two beautiful girls, a one-year-old and a five-year-old. She was homeless. Sans apartment and house, she was broke. Did she compromise, turn to her own devices? Did she take matters into her own hands since God apparently was sleeping at the wheel or simply did not care?

No. She trusted her God and amazing things happened. The little, poor church she attended found out this incredibly godly young single mom, who was busy serving others, was homeless. They all, and I mean *all*, pooled their meager resources, bought a badly conditioned mobile home and began the two-week marathon to rehab it so that Rain and her two girls could have a place to stay off the streets. We found out a few days before they were finished and decided to film the project. What we found shook us to the core. I still cannot imagine or fathom what took place.

Rain is overwhelmingly generous and unlike anyone I have ever met. Her friend, a hair-cutter, was diagnosed with breast cancer. Rain wanted to give her something, something from her heart, something valuable and precious. The problem was she had nothing. Well, she did have one thing—long, beautiful hair.

The chemo and radiation had ravaged her friend and she was bald. Being a woman without hair is extremely difficult. A hairdresser without hair is worse. Rain wanted her friend to have dignity, so she cut her own hair so that her friend could have a wig. A homeless, single mom took her eyes off of her own situation and considered someone else's dilemma as being more important. What is the really strange part? The act was a joyful one for Rain and one that paid happiness dividends way beyond her expectation.

While filming the people working on Rain's new home, I saw the recipient of the hair. I approached cautiously. I could not wait to ask her questions about the cancer and Rain and the church, but I didn't want to scare her with my excitement. She patiently answered all my eagerly posed questions. I asked her what she was doing at the mobile home along with the other volunteers at the church. She said her husband was doing the flooring and that he had not been to church for quite a while because the pastor of his old church had borrowed money from church members and then ran away with all of it.

I wince when I hear this and similar stories of such godless men who will be judged so severely.[110] But as we were running the camera (see www.account417.com for this interview), her husband said that he had never seen a church do something like this. He saw a group of believers that was truly sincere in showing others who their God is. He decided then that he would like to start going to this church. He is now one of the key leaders there.

Rain trusted God for a house. She was busy serving instead of stewing. What can you trust God with?

DAY 47

Margin and Meaning

"... I AM CARRYING ON A GREAT PROJECT AND CANNOT GO DOWN ... ."
(NEHEMIAH 6:3)

"MORE PEOPLE ARE BRIBED BY THEIR OWN MONEY THAN
ANYBODY ELSE'S." – JONATHAN DANIELS

"IF WE CONSIDER THE UNBLUSHING PROMISES OF REWARD AND THE
STAGGERING NATURE OF THE REWARDS PROMISED IN THE GOSPELS, IT
WOULD SEEM THAT OUR LORD FINDS OUR DESIRE NOT TOO STRONG, BUT
TOO WEAK. WE ARE HALF-HEARTED CREATURES, FOOLING ABOUT WITH
DRINK AND SEX AND AMBITION WHEN INFINITE JOY IS OFFERED US, WE
ARE LIKE IGNORANT CHILDREN WHO WANT TO CONTINUE MAKING MUD
PIES IN A SLUM BECAUSE WE CANNOT IMAGINE WHAT IS MEANT BY THE
OFFER OF A VACATION AT THE SEA. WE ARE FAR TOO EASILY PLEASED."
– C.S. LEWIS

Do it His way! His way means more of both margin and meaning. Simply put, margin is what we save and meaning is what we spend. Our significance is found in spending. Show me your checkbook and I will tell you definitively where your significance lies. The problem is that the places and the things most people spend their money, time, talents, and energy on are not meaningful. Finding one's significance in things is temporary. That is why you must keep buying, keep spending, keep upgrading, because the thing or things you just bought will not satisfy for long. The American dream and the ideals of getting bigger, better, and more are not easily reconcilable with Christianity.

When you get to Heaven, do you think God is going to say, "Wow, millions died without knowing Me on your watch, but that fountain outside your house was gorgeous. And I loved your Hummer and centralized vacuum system. People saw those things and instantly dropped to their knees and gave their lives to Me." Do you think anyone will come up to you and say, "I was orphaned when my parents starved to death, but your big-screen TV was my saving grace. Thank you."

This is not to say that having things is bad, but some perspective is needed. When simply owning a car puts you in the elite 8 percent of the world's population, does having a BMW seem as important? When the world's health and education needs could be wiped out with the dollar amount that Americans spend each year on ice cream, does having the very best seem as satisfying? Always remember, *our* world is not *the* world.[111]

The God-given desire for satisfaction will wrestle with our hearts and minds until we temper that desire, this time hoping to have long-term satisfaction. Then we find that we must anesthetize our hearts once again, and when the satisfaction wanes, Madison Avenue is quick to offer a new fix to inject into our hearts and bring us a very transitory joy.

As long as the money holds out and the series of injections continue, we will stay on that roller coaster, until we choose one of three paths. One, the path of the *enlightened* who saw this path of destruction and decided death was far better, two, the holders of *hope* who, even if logically futile, merely continue on with this destructive and meaningless lifestyle of spending and consuming, or three, those who choose to leave the destructive path and believe that there is a God who loves them deeply and is waiting for them right now with open arms, without rolling His eyes or shaking His head.[112]

His nail-scarred hands are outstretched, a testament to the sacrifice He welcomed in order to save our souls from death in hell and to give us a life on this planet that is truly rich. Not the wimpy, unsatisfying riches of money and consumerism, but true, altruistic contentedness.[113]

If we could take a step back, take a look at our lives, and eschew the worldly wisdom that bigger is better, we would see our path could never satisfy. His path is the only one that truly satisfies. That is why Nehemiah chose such an endeavor, gave up so much in the earthly sense, because he knew that what he gave up paled in comparison to the eternal greatness of following the path God had for him.

Here are some steps to take:

1st - Surrender: God, I will do it your way from now on; I surrender this part of my life that I have been holding back. (Remember Nehemiah's prayer in Chapter 1:5-12.)

2nd - Come clean: Just stop it! Do it His way and you will avoid financial pain. It's old school. It's called obedience.[114]

3rd - Get out of debt, stay out of debt: Tell those people who say that debt is good that 1.8 billion people in the world live on one dollar or less a day, and one dies every second from hunger. If those folks really, truly cared about life they wouldn't give another cent to the credit card companies in interest. They would invest in people's lives.

4th - Start saving: Again, obedience.

5th - Get serious about investing: Not for the next forty years. I am talking about serious, intelligent investing; the kind of investing that saves lives. The money entrusted to us can either bring people to know God in a deeper way or send people to their deaths and many to hell. We can use money for our pleasures, comfort, and keeping up with the Joneses, but this nauseating life just gets more and more crazy as we continue on the treadmill of debt. Or we can use money to glorify Him.

This runs completely contrary to conventional financial wisdom and that is why I love it so much. If the world is so good at handling money, why aren't there more content, satisfied people who are chasing money as a way of life? I call them financial hedonists—seeking money and what money can acquire as a way of life. Much different from the Christian hedonist, as John Piper coins it, "My shortest summary of Christian hedonism is: God is most glorified in us when we are most satisfied in Him."

God's idea of financial hedonism is found in multiple places in His Scriptures. The Apostle Paul wrote a letter to Timothy and basically said to him, "Tell those with more money than they need to not put their trust and hope in it because, frankly, you can't trust money. You never know what may happen to it, but trust God, and remember it is okay to enjoy it as gift from God. But if you want great joy, the joy that will last through this life and throughout eternity, the amount of money you have been entrusted with can show people who your God is, and will bring people to know Him. Thus, people will be going to Heaven instead of hell because of your generosity."

So upgrade your desires today.

DAY 48

Lord, I Need Strength!

"... But I prayed, 'Now strengthen my hands.'" (Nehemiah 6:9)

"I asked God for strength that I might achieve. I was made weak that I might learn humbly to obey. I asked for health that I might do greater things. I was given infirmity that I might do better things. I asked for riches that I might be happy. I was given poverty that I might be wise. I asked for power that I might have the praise of men. I was given weakness that I might feel the need of God. I asked for all things that I might enjoy life. I was given life that I might enjoy all things. I got nothing that I asked for, but everything I hoped for. Almost despite myself, my unspoken prayers were answered. I am, among all men, most richly blessed." – Unknown

"Not everything that can be counted counts, and not everything that counts can be counted." – Albert Einstein

This is a prayer of a "man's man." A prayer that is not wimpy or full of fear. This one was a prayer to the God of finishing—the God who could give the extra push at the end to allow us to make it. That push can only come from God.

It wasn't the prayer of the coward: "Rescue me, God, from the bad people and I will go to church every Sunday, and give a few extra bucks for Your cause. I need You this time and I will never forget You. I'll even be kind to my mother-in-law."

I can just hear God saying, "Now that's my kind of prayer, baby. Now that you've got my attention, do you want Me to fetch a stick while I'm at it?"

Well, this was certainly the time for Nehemiah. The contract had already been taken out on his head.

That is the score; you are close to finishing your fortress. You might say, "I am not out of debt, or rich, or married yet; how could my fortress be a few days from finishing?" By following God's plan your financial fortress will be impenetrable.

But right now you may be feeling like a good friend of mine whose wife of almost thirty years went to be with the Lord after a lengthy battle with cancer. The first question we ask is why? They are such a godly couple, raising three godly children and making an impact in countless lives. The last chapter has not been written.

His heart longs for his sweetheart and sometimes he feels he does not have the strength to go on. But as a tribute to his wife, he chooses to invest in the lives of those who have never heard the life-changing message of Jesus Christ who was crucified out of love for a lost world. You can make it, Mark; just a little bit longer. We can almost hear Jody cheering you and the kids on.

Your hands may be bloody, but your prayer is one of strength. Though it may be impossible to appreciate a rose when you are bleeding, you can still know the hand of God is always there.

Nehemiah's courage was focused on the only sure thing in the universe. Your financial fortress is built not on merely paying off your credit card debt or paying off the mortgage or saving for a house or car or even achieving radical Nehemiah generosity, but knowing that complete trust and obedience in God is rich and effortless.

No matter where we are financially, whether well fed or hungry, whether having money or not, we can know the secret of being content. Paul wrote a letter to the followers of Christ, some of them former soldiers, in Philippi, Greece, while he was in prison to thank them and to encourage them. Toward the end of that book, Philippians 4, he said he had learned the secret of being content. He could be happy in any situation because he could do anything through Christ who was giving him the strength to go on. He then says in verse 17 that his goal is not to receive a reward from them, but for them to gain as much as possible of the things that are eternal.

You will be able to look back at this time and know that God never left you. But perhaps you are still unconvinced because the pain is so great. You need to share your situation with a financial coach or counselor. Please don't end up like my friend, a great and talented physician, but one with great financial heartache. Dr. Wing decided to jump off the balcony of his 17th story condo on South Beach. I knew there were financial problems and wanted to help, but the pain was so great that he traded God's solution for a deceptive and tragic ending.

If you remember only one thing from this book, remember that God has an incredible plan for your life and that we all can finish well.

DAY 49

Compromise This!

" ... SHOULD A MAN LIKE ME RUN AWAY? ..." (NEHEMIAH 6:11)

"COMPLETE POSSESSION IS PROVED ONLY BY GIVING. ALL YOU ARE
UNABLE TO GIVE POSSESSES YOU." – ANDRE GIDE

"PRUDENCE AND COMPROMISE ARE NECESSARY MEANS, BUT EVERY MAN
SHOULD HAVE AN IMPUDENT END WHICH HE WILL NOT COMPROMISE."
– CHARLES HORTON COOLEY

Nehemiah was nearly blindsided and rammed with a fatal blow. Almost at the end of the amazing re-construction, he was at a priest's house.[115] The man of the cloth informed him that his life was in danger and pleaded with him to hide in a temple.

Not a bad idea, actually. No one with any character or sense would go into this sacred place and look for someone to kill. That would be disastrous. Only the priest was allowed in the Temple building itself.[116] Actually, it could be a bad idea to hide in the Temple for the same reason. As a matter of fact, years earlier a king by the name of Uzziah went into the Temple to burn some incense and he was punished with leprosy.[117]

Nehemiah knew his history and knew his God even better. He was not going to run. If this was his time, so be it. If God had taken him this far just to allow him to die a martyr's death, he was ready. Jesus Christ said, "I tell you the truth, unless a kernel of wheat falls to the ground and dies, it remains only a single seed. But if it dies, it produces many seeds."[118]

Nehemiah was bold in the face of death. We can likewise be bold in the face of imminent financial death.

I was facing clear and convincing financial devastation at twenty-one. Bankruptcy was absolutely the only option. No one wanted the five-dollars-a month-payment I could make until I was able to save up enough to fully pay what I had borrowed or stolen. I wasn't really running; I was taking advantage of the laws of the United States Bankruptcy Code. It was only to get me on my feet and then I would pay it off later. At least that's what I told myself.

But David's words in Psalm 37:21, "The wicked borrow and do not repay but the righteous give generously... ." rang louder than the world's undertone. I chose to face the creditors, this time not alone, but with my advocate—God—by my side. I trusted Him to rescue and comfort me throughout the worst that could befall me. He never left me and within five years of my fall, and one month before getting married, I became debt free! Dave Ramsey could have heard me scream, "Freedom!" without a telephone or microphone in 1993.

I could have run when I was arrested, I could have jumped bond when on bail, I could have skipped out on the creditors, but God had a better, more satisfying, joy-giving plan that included a second chance. If I had listened to the voice of compromise I would have never known the pure and intense pleasure that only knowing and trusting Him provides. I am so incredibly glad He nudged me in that direction.

He is nudging you right now.

It is absolutely amazing how in the eleventh hour the evil one tells his lies. The solution may be to just run, file bankruptcy, short-sell your real estate, and not leave a forwarding address. What about the money? It will probably be written it off anyway. After all, God has given you a brain, so do whatever it takes, whatever feels right. Right? That is not the way Nehemiah did it. He trusted the God who had brought him this far. Will you?

DAY 50

Bold Prayers

"REMEMBER TOBIAH AND SANBALLAT, O MY GOD, BECAUSE OF WHAT
THEY HAVE DONE... ." (NEHEMIAH 6:14)

"THE REAL MEASURE OF YOUR WEALTH IS HOW MUCH YOU'D BE WORTH
IF YOU LOST ALL YOUR MONEY." – UNKNOWN

"WHAT DIFFERENCE DOES IT MAKE HOW MUCH YOU HAVE? WHAT YOU
DO NOT HAVE AMOUNTS TO MUCH MORE." – SENECA

Nehemiah dodged a bullet. Now he was back to his Father's business. But first things first. He needed a conference call ASAP. He went directly to the CEO, the chief, the foreman: God. It wasn't a strong, fearless prayer because he was inches away from losing it.

God took this emotional, yet levelheaded, wine taster to the edge of the miraculous and back. Nehemiah had to pour out his emotional heart to his God first, though.

Imagine a prayer starting with the word, "Remember." We usually begin prayers to a big God with the words: "Dear God," or "O God," or "God, I know you're out there... ." But Nehemiah got into the habit of asking God to remember the things that had just taken place.

It is a bold prayer not many of us are man enough to pray. It is not exactly the way Jesus taught us to pray either.[119] There was, however, something very rich and transparent and honest about this prayer. It wasn't a threat, a "Bless me or else" prayer, or a selfish "Please give me a Lexus" prayer. It was a prayer that a son has with a dad who loves him and is interested in what he has to say.

It was a mature, yet childlike prayer that showed Nehemiah's spiritual maturity even during life-threatening, adrenaline-filled moments. It exemplified the type of relationship that would not be jeopardized by the plea of a son who simply asked his dad to remember what sacrifice he has faced and the good he has done, and the evil that others have tried to do.

Nehemiah asked the Creator of the universe to remember the wicked lies that the three stooges had told. They would not give in and go away. Their lot in life was to make Nehemiah miserable and try to kill him as a bonus. "Remember Tobiah and Sanballat, O my God, because of what they have done."

Your situation might be exactly the same. We have all faced betrayal, backstabbing, or someone who has hurt us so badly that even to this day it is unspeakable. What if we were able to have a friend that was so close, so in love with us that we could actually say anything that came to mind? Nehemiah did. He was a friend of his Father's.

It is time to bring those who are seeking to break down your financial fortress to the attention of your best friend and shoot straight with Him. There are so many financial temptations that we lose track. From the credit card applications in your mail, the re-finance email from your bank, the telemarketer that somehow always gets through your "no call list," to the really big temptations found while watching your favorite reality show on cable.

Bring them to Him and remember those things you have been overcome by in the past and flee from them. Go to your closet and thank God you have such cool stuff. Try some on and appreciate what you have and maybe share some with others as you are thinking about it.

This is one of the greatest things Nehemiah did in Jerusalem. He made sure all the residents shared with others often. It was a lifestyle that kept things in perspective. We are rich and we can bring a blessing to others who do not have what we do. This produces great joy.

You remember when you fell in love. You couldn't wait to chat, whatever the method: letter, email, iChat, IM, text messaging, telephone. You could say whatever was on your mind. That communication brought the relationship to another level, a level that created a bond that released a trust that satisfied an innate desire, a longing everyone has, but not all are able to experience. Nehemiah had that type of openness with God. It was as natural as breathing and just as satisfying.

When you have this kind of relationship, you pray like Nehemiah.

DAY 51

I Am Willing

"THEY WERE HOPING TO INTIMIDATE ME... ." (NEHEMIAH 6:13, NLT)

"BEING WILLING MAKES YOU ABLE." – RHONDA BRITTEN

"POSSESSION DIMINISHES PERCEPTION OF VALUE, IMMEDIATELY."
– JOHN UPDIKE

Those three small words changed Nehemiah's life and legacy forever, and they can change yours, too.

Nehemiah's life could have been snuffed out by his enemies had God allowed it. Even so, his life demonstrated the power and the hope that only comes from obedience and complete dependence on the Creator. In the words of David, an earlier king after God's own heart, "Some trust in chariots and some in horses, but we trust in the name of the Lord our God."[120] By his actions he said, "I am willing." As a result, Nehemiah's story of complete trust in God has made him and his God an example to hundreds of millions, perhaps billions, of people who have read God's Word spoken through his writing.

Chet Bitterman was willing, perfectly willing, to trust God to share the "Good News."[121] So valuable was the message of the greatness and glory of God, he wrote in his journal just before arriving in Colombia, "... I find the recurring thought that perhaps God will call me to be martyred for Him in His service in Colombia. *I am willing.*"

Guerrillas stormed the mission guesthouse, looking for a high-ranking leader of Wycliffe Bible Translators to further

161

their evil cause. Instead, they got a young, twenty-nine-year-old who managed the guesthouse, who was buying food and goods needed by other mission workers. But his desire was to move into the jungle with the Carijona Indian tribe to translate the Bible so that these people could have the Word of God in their language. His captors had a markedly different agenda.

On January 19, 1981, just one day before President Ronald Reagan took the oath of office and the American hostages in Iran were released after 444 days in captivity, Chet's ordeal of willingness was just beginning. The terrorists demanded two things: that their views be printed in the world's leading newspapers and that all Wycliffe mission workers leave Colombia in thirty days or Chet would die.

Chet and Wycliffe were not willing to exit Colombia until the work of translating the Bible in every language was complete. Chet's wife, Brenda, and their two toddlers prayed, hoped, and waited. They prayed that Chet would remember God's Word. A letter was released from Chet that spoke of the great hope he derived from the stories of others in difficult situations like Paul and Daniel's three friends, Shadrach, Meshach, and Abednego. He stated, "In the case of Daniel's friends, God did something very unusual through His power for a specific purpose, so that through everything, all concerned would learn about Him." He ended his letter with this line, "Wouldn't it be neat if something special like this would happen?"

Something special would happen. The media printed Chet's letter in its entirety, Scripture references and all. God had already begun getting His Word out. Forty-eight days after Chet was abducted, on the morning of March 7, a bullet to his chest ended Chet's life. His limp body was later discovered on a city bus. When his parents were interviewed after his death, Chet's father said, "I'm sorry I won't see Chet again in this life but I know I'll see him again in Heaven." His dad then spoke of the love Chet, his mother, and he shared for the Colombian people. His mom stated, "We're hoping the guerrillas come to know God."

As Chet was lowered into a grave in the Columbian city he loved, at memorial services all over the world men and women stepped forward to take Chet's place and answer the call to full-time, dangerous frontier missionary service. Applications to Wycliffe skyrocketed in the months after Chet's death.

God calls us to live this same willingness in our own lives. Your Columbia may be your workplace, your church, or even your home, but the job application remains the same. Be willing.

DAY 52

They Finished

"So the wall was completed on the twenty-fifth of Elul, in
fifty-two days."(Nehemiah 6:15)

"Here is the test to find whether your mission on Earth is
finished. If you're alive, it isn't." – Richard Bach

"Lo, I am with you always... ." (Matthew 28:20, KJV)

Nehemiah had been looking forward to this day throughout
his whole life. True, it was only fifty-two days in the making
and it was an incredible miracle to see it accomplished in
such a short time. The defining moment happened on the 25th
of Elul in the Hebrew lunar calendar; on ours it would have
been October 2, 445 B.C. That day, when the naysayers were
silenced, the Earth must have seemed to stand still in perfect
celestial order.[122]

Before the celebration and thanksgiving were destined to
take place, complete with hugs and kisses and tears, it was a day
of reckoning for those who wanted harm to befall these hard-
working, God–fearing, perfume makers, business people, kids,
laborers, pastors, and just regular Joes. Now it was a little bit
of God-orchestrated pay-back time.

When their enemies heard that the fortress was completed
in fifty-two days, it is reported that all the surrounding nations
were afraid and lost their self-confidence, because they realized
that this had been an act of a powerful God, the God of the
universe. These are the same people that could have squashed

them. The bad guys outnumbered them, were more powerful, and were better trained, but they did not have Almighty God on their side. As a matter of fact, they were fighting God and when you fight God, you lose. They lost confidence because their confidence was in themselves.

God had a victory that topped all victories that day. And now it was time to thank the One who stuck by them through thick and thin, the One who is closer than a brother.[123] A truer friend no one has ever had. If we have such a friend, we are unstoppable.

You have traveled down this trail for fifty-two days. Now it is time to celebrate God's goodness. Perhaps you are looking at your financial fortress and thinking, "I want more of this success, more of this partnership, more of this Friend who sticks closer than a brother."

I welcome you to continue. Nehemiah did not go back to his day job and send everyone home after the fifty-two days to forget about the city. That was just the end of Chapter 6 of the story and there were seven more chapters to go. The wall was built by regular people who were not builders by any stretch of the imagination. They proved they could trust God into the next phase of construction. Their confidence rose, not in themselves, like their enemies who were scattered, but in their God.

Nehemiah and his not-ready-for-prime-time contractors are now in Heaven looking down, cheering you on. "A great cloud of witnesses" surrounds us. Those who have gone before us and now are rooting us on, cheering for us, telling us we can do it.[124] The word "witnesses" is translated from the English word "martyr." So picture this truth: you are surrounded literally by a huge cloud of martyrs that have seen and experienced the amazing power of faith in God and they are cheering for you.

You now have the fortress complete in a faith-building, record-setting time. The fortress is not brick and mortar, it is not your finances; it is a fortress of faith. A spiritual stalwart that will repel any attack the world can muster. Now continue.

Finishing well begins with celebrating well. Six days after the fortress was finished, on October 8th (our calendar), it was time for a party. The guest of honor was none other than the One who made it all possible, the One who performed the miracles, the One who forgave and showed such lovingkindness. And now everyone was ready to celebrate the accomplishment.[125] Guess what they did on the way to the party? They brought gifts. Sure, every woman remembers to bring a gift to a party, but most of us men figure it's no big deal. But the governor set the stage by giving 19 pounds (8.6 kilos) of gold and some other valuables. The others gave another 750 pounds (340 kilos) of gold, and 5,250 pounds of silver.

That was an astounding display of sacrifice. In today's US dollars, 348.6 kilos of gold at over $21,000 per kilo totals over $7.3 million. The silver today is worth another $1 million. Can you imagine that offering, pastors? Your people better know CPR or there are going to be lots of folks entering the pearly gates on that day.

Nehemiah was surrounded by godly people. Ezra, the priest, read God's Word.[126] The masses of people took to their feet and listened attentively as Ezra praised the Lord, the great God, and then it erupted. All the people started to raise their hands, and they could not help but say, "Amen, Amen!"

Then, in an awe-inspiring gesture of the ultimate in humility of worship, they fell prostrate with their faces on the ground. Can you imagine that scene? Almost 50,000 people on the ground worshipping God? It sounds like a Promise Keepers event, but this time I am sure, after working together for fifty-two days, the emotional bonds were so deep that a half-day festival of worship was quite a satisfying aroma to the God of Heaven.

Just when you thought it couldn't get any better, Nehemiah, along with all of the pastors, explained the meaning of the Word of God so clearly that everyone understood. This tactic could put some clergy out of business today. But it was God's desire.

The emotions ran high that day. They gave, they heard, they understood (some perhaps for the first time), they worshiped, they mourned, and they wept. Then the leaders told the people that today was a very sacred day to the Lord; don't cry any longer for the joy of the Lord is and will be the strength you need to take the next step.[127]

Now it is your turn. You may feel like the people did in Nehemiah's day. You are spent; you can't make it. Remember the words of Nehemiah as he spoke to the people in chapter 8, verse 10, "Go and enjoy choice food and sweet drinks, and send some to those who have nothing prepared. This day is sacred to our Lord. Do not grieve, for the joy of the Lord is your strength." You don't have to muster up enough strength to make it; God will take it from here. And remember to share with those who are homeless, single moms, or folks who are just plain struggling with one thing or another, without regard for whether or not they may have made bad choices. God is still there for us when we make bad choices. Let us share with joy and without finding fault. If we all do this, we may just enter into His joy.

I, along with those who have gone before us, cheer you on to victory and the sweet taste of true riches.[128] That is the tapping into the life that is truly life![129]

"I TELL YOU, USE WORLDLY WEALTH TO GAIN FRIENDS FOR YOURSELVES, SO THAT WHEN IT IS GONE, YOU WILL BE WELCOMED INTO ETERNAL DWELLINGS." – JESUS CHRIST (AS QUOTED IN LUKE 16:9)

The Nehemiah Challenge

Take the Nehemiah challenge. We call it the *417 Challenge*.[130] Nehemiah experienced a wealth that was literally out this world. He did not value the things the world did, but valued what God valued.

The challenge is this: if you are ready to upgrade and do it God's way, and live each day with eternity in view, practicing Philippians 4:17 and Nehemiah 5:9, considering others more important than yourself and looking for what they will gain, then do it. You see, doing it God's way is not only right, but also smart, and dare I say *selfish*, because the joy in seeing someone else's life change is the greatest joy ever created by God!

If you do take the *417 Challenge*, let us know and we will send you a free survival kit. It is the same kit you receive when you come to one of our events. Just go to www.account417.com and send us an email with your address and we will mail it out at no cost to you.

Live Original!

Endnotes

1   Jeremiah 29:11
2   Romans 15:13

Day 1

3   See Biblegateway.com
4   Proverbs 10:22

Day 2

5   See our video Drinking the American Dream
6   http://nl.newsbank.com/nl-search/we/Archives?p_product=MH&s_
     site=miami&p_multi=MH&p_theme=realcities&p_
     action=search&p_maxdocs=200&p_topdoc=1&p_text_direct-
     0=0EB367D7282900F0&p_field_direct-0=document_id&p_
     perpage=10&p_sort=YMD_date:D&s_trackval=GooglePM

Day 3

7   According to tradition, Isaiah the prophet was sawn in half by the
     wicked King Manassah (see *NIV Study Bible*, note for Hebrews
     11:37)
8   Isaiah 42:3
9   Eighty percent of marriages that end in divorce and 50 percent of
     suicides are caused by financial distress.

Day 4

10   Nehemiah 1:4-7
11   Proverbs 23:23
12   Psalm 24:1, Psalm 50:9-12

Day 5

13   List the sources of commentaries reviewed
14   Nehemiah 1:9
15   James 4:2-3

Day 6

16 Like the words that were spoken to Esther by her cousin Mordecai approximately thirty years earlier, around 460 B.C., "For if you remain silent at this time relief and deliverance for the Jews will arise from another place, but you and your father's family will perish. And who knows but that you have come to royal position for such a time as this." As stated in Esther 4:14, NIV

17 Henry David Thoreau in *Walden* observes his neighbors breaking their backs to make money and get ahead and so fulfill their lives.

18 I Corinthians 6:19-20

Day 7

19 Nehemiah 1:4, Ecclesiastes 12:13, Psalms 84:11b

Day 8

20 Nehemiah's memoirs were around 430 B.C., while Joshua's feats were in 1250 B.C.

21 Joshua 24:1

22 Psalm 103:5

23 Joshua 24:15b

24 Joshua 24:18b

Day 9

25 Nehemiah 1:11

26 Psalm 81:11b

Day 10

27 Nehemiah took a leave of absence in the twentieth year of the King's reign (Nehemiah 2:1) and was still granted this privilege twelve years later as he kept tabs on the nicely built and maintained city. (Nehemiah 13:5)

Day 11

28 Proverbs 3:5

29 II Chronicles 6:30 and I Kings 8:39; Psalm 84:11b

Day 12

30 Romans 5:8; John 15:13

31 Nehemiah 2:4

32 Nehemiah 2:5a
33 Psalm 42:2
34 Romans 15:13

Day 13
35 Lake of Gennesaret is also known as the Sea of Galilee, the Sea of Tiberias, and Lake Kinneret. It is still to this day the most important water resource in Israel and provides more than 35 percent of the country's drinking water. It is the only freshwater lake in the country. See study athttp://www.uwa.edu.au/media/statements/2001/07/uwa_research_underway_at_the_sea_of_galilee_(6_july)
36 Luke 5:8

Day 14
37 Mammon: The spirit of the love of money. Contrary to what Suze Orman says about money having power, it does not; but money in the hands of people can have great power. That power can bring or preserve life or take life; we have that choice.

Day 15
38 Nehemiah 2:6
39 Nehemiah 2:20

Day 16
40 Nehemiah 2:11-12

Day 17
41 Nehemiah 2:10
42 Joel 3:3 and Obadiah 11
43 See Voice of the Martyrs@persecution.com

Day 18
44 Nehemiah 2:17
45 Haggai 2:8

Day 19
46 *Live Original* is our battle cry
47 Proverbs 16:3
48 James 4:3

Day 20

49 Psalm 51 chronicles David's pain in living a lie.
50 The words of Isaiah in Isaiah 42:3 & Matthew 12:20
51 *Working the Room*, by Nick Morgan; Harvard Business School Press Copyright 2003

Day 21

52 Nehemiah 4:12
53 www.globalissues.org

Day 22

54 Proverbs 3:5

Day 23

55 Twenty-six times in the Hebrew Scriptures it is written that He will not leave us nor forsake us and for us to be strong and courageous.

Day 24

56 See actual footage of this video at www.52days.com
57 Isaiah 55:11

Day 25

58 Pastor of the First Baptist Church of Atlanta; father of Andy Stanley.
59 *Live Original* is our battle cry

Day 26

60 (http://www.moneyandhappiness.com/blog/?cat=43)
61 Nehemiah 3:5
62 Luke 21:1-4
63 Actually not even that much; she put into the temple treasury two minas, half of penny each, thus see put in one cent.
64 Twenty-two times in God's Word we are told that God will never leave us or forsake us, and that we can be strong and courageous

Day 27

65 Nehemiah 3:14

Day 28

66 Nehemiah 4:4

Day 30

67 Twenty-six times in God's Word do we hear this promise that He will never leave us nor forsake us and that we should be strong and courageous.
68 Revelation 21:8
69 Nehemiah 4:14
70 Nehemiah 4:15

Day 31

71 The AP-AOL Health poll involved telephone interviews with 1,002 adults from all states except Alaska and Hawaii and was conducted from March 24 to April 3, 2008 by Abt SRBI Inc. The margin of sampling error was plus or minus 3.1 percentage points. See http://www.foxnews.com/printer_friendly_story/0,3566,364581,00.html
72 Matthew 11:28-29, MSG

Day 32

73 *Don't Waste Your Life*, By John Piper, published by Crossway Books 2007
74 Esther 4:14
75 Matthew 11:28-30, MSG

Day 33

76 Charles Stanley once was moved to sell his most valuable earthly possession—his cameras in order to invest in the lives of people at the First Baptist Church of Atlanta.
77 Genesis 22: 1-18

Day 34

78 Philippians 2:3-4
78 Romans 13:8

Day 35

79 Proverbs 13:11b
80 Deuteronomy 23:20
81 Exodus 22:25-27

82 Philippians 4:19:"And my God will meet all your needs according his glorious riches in Christ Jesus."
83 Quoted from Antiquities 4.8.25
84 The opposite of Solomon's words in Proverbs 3:5-6

Day 36

85 Philippians 3:19
86 Philippians 3:20
87 *The Lion, the Witch, and the Wardrobe —The Chronicles of Narnia*
88 Psalm 84:11

Day 37

89 *How Much Land Does A Man Need?* (1886) by Leo Tolstoy, translated by Louise and Aylmer Maude.
90 See previous foot note.
91 This is considered plausible by some commentators but the fact that Nehemiah had to request to rebuild the city and risked rejection by the king adds a shadow of doubt to whether Artaxerxes was in fact Esther's benefactor.
92 Luke 16:11
93 I Timothy 6:19
94 Joshua 24:14-27

Day 38

95 Luke 16:11
96 Luke 16:9
97 Nehemiah 5:19
98 The meat mentioned here in verse 18 would provide 600-800 meals per day.

Day 39

99 According to a Barna poll, those who profess faith in Christ as Savior, etc.
100 www.1040window.org

Day 40

101 George Muller, *The Autobiography of George Muller*, (Whitaker House, 1984, page 161.)
102 Philippians 4:11-13

Day 41
103 *The Autobiography of George Muller,* (Whitaker House, © 1985, page 140.)

Day 42
104 Agur, son of Jakeh, was a wise man like Ethan and Heman; See I Kings 4:31, and probably a descendant of Ishmael, thus a non-Israelite background (from NIV Study Note)
105 www.crown.org/LIBRARY/ViewArticle.aspx?ArticleId=405
106 www.globalissues.org
107 Luke 16:9

Day 43
108 Nehemiah 6:3

Day 44
109 II Corinthians 6:10

Day 46
110 Jude 4-16

Day 47
111 http://www.globalissues.org/TradeRelated/Facts.asp
112 "For you, Lord, are good, and ready to forgive, and abundant in loving-kindness to all who call upon You"(Psalm 86:5, NASB)
113 Luke 16:11; Ecclesiastes 5:11
114 Nehemiah 1:6, Proverbs 10:22, and Romans 15:13

Day 49
115 Nehemiah 6:10
116 Numbers 18:7
117 2 Chronicles 26:16-21
118 John 12:24

Day 50
119 Matthew 6 and Luke 11

Day 51
120 Psalm 20:7

121 Chester A. "Chet" Bitterman III (1952-1981) missionary martyr to Colombia with Wycliffe Bible Translators

Day 52

122 Nehemiah 6:15
123 Proverbs 18:24
124 Hebrews 12:1
125 There were 49,942 people to be exact; plus 736 horses, 245 mules, 435 camels, and 6720 donkeys. (Nehemiah 7:66-69)
126 Nehemiah 8:2-7
127 Nehemiah 8:9-10
128 Luke 16:11
129 I Timothy 6:19

The Nehemiah Challenge

130 www.account417.com